Do-it Yourself
BASICS

Save Money • Solve Problems • Improve Your Home

THE BASICS EVERYONE CAN MASTER

Reader's Digest

New York, NY/Montreal

Do-It Yourself Basics

Content Management Mary Flanagan
Design Elizabeth Tunnicliffe
Page Layout David Farr
Proofreader Judy Arginteanu

Text, photography and illustrations for *Do-It Yourself Basics* are based on articles previously published in *The Family Handyman* magazine (2915 Commers Dr., Suite 700, Eagan, MN 55121, familyhandyman.com). For information on advertising in *The Family Handyman* magazine, call (646) 518-4215.

Do-It Yourself Basics is published by Trusted Media Brands, Inc. ©2019

Family Handyman ISBN: 978-1-62145-433-5
Family Handyman ISBN: 978-1-62145-431-1
Reader's Digest ISBN: 978-1-62145-432-8

Address any comments to:
feedback@familyhandyman.com

A Note to Our Readers

All do-it-yourself activities involve a degree of risk. Skills, materials, tools and site conditions vary widely. Although the editors have made every effort to ensure accuracy, the reader remains responsible for the selection and use of tools, materials and methods. Always obey local codes and laws, follow manufacturer instructions and observe safety precautions.

Pricing

Professional services and supplies can vary widely depending on the market. Those listed are average costs and are just a guide to cost savings.

The Family Handyman

EDITORIAL
Chief Content Officer Nick Grzechowiak
Editor in Chief Gary Wentz
Senior Editors Mary Flanagan, Travis Larson, Mark Petersen,
Associate Editors Mike Berner, Brad Holden, Josh Risberg
Managing Editor Donna Bierbach
Assistant Editors Matt Boley, Elizabeth Flaherty, Harrison Kral
Contributing Copy Editor Peggy Parker
Contributing Editors Spike Carlsen, Rick Muscoplat, April Wilkerson
Lead Carpenter Jeremiah James
Editorial Services Associate Peggy McDermott

ART
Associate Creative Director Vern Johnson
Senior Designer Marcia Roepke
Graphic Designer Mariah Cates
Production Artist Mary Schwender
Photographer Tom Fenenga

Trusted Media Brands, Inc.
President & Chief Executive Officer
Bonnie Kintzer

PRINTED IN CHINA

1 2 3 4 5 6 7 8 9 10

Safety first – always!

Tackling home improvement projects and repairs can be endlessly rewarding.
But as most of us know, with the rewards come risks.
The good news is, armed with the right knowledge, tools and procedures, homeowners
can minimize risk. As you go about your projects and repairs, stay alert for these hazards:

Aluminum wiring

Aluminum wiring, installed in about 7 million homes between 1965 and 1973, requires special techniques and materials to make safe connections. This wiring is dull gray, not the dull orange characteristic of copper. Hire a licensed electrician certified to work with it. For more information go to cpsc.gov and search for "aluminum wiring."

Spontaneous combustion

Rags saturated with oil finishes like Danish oil and linseed oil, and oil-based paints and stains can spontaneously combust if left bunched up. Always dry them outdoors, spread out loosely. When the oil has thoroughly dried, you can safely throw them in the trash.

Vision and hearing protection

Safety glasses or goggles should be worn whenever you're working on DIY projects that involve chemicals, dust and anything that could shatter or chip off and hit your eye. Sounds louder than 80 decibels (dB) are considered potentially dangerous. Sound levels from a lawn mower can be 90 dB, and shop tools and chain saws can be 90 to 100 dB.

Lead paint

If your home was built before 1979, it may contain lead paint, which is a serious health hazard, especially for children 6 and under. Take precautions when you scrape or remove it. Contact your public health department for detailed safety information or call (800) 424-LEAD (5323) to receive an information pamphlet. Or visit epa.gov/lead.

Buried utilities

A few days before you dig in your yard, have your underground water, gas and electrical lines marked. Just call 811 or go to call811.com.

Smoke and carbon monoxide (CO) alarms

The risk of dying in reported home structure fires is cut in half in homes with working smoke alarms. Test your smoke alarms every month, replace batteries as necessary and replace units that are more than 10 years old. As you make your home more energy-efficient and airtight, existing ducts and chimneys can't always successfully vent combustion gases, including potentially deadly carbon monoxide (CO). Install a UL-listed CO detector, and test your CO and smoke alarms at the same time.

Five-gallon buckets and window covering cords

From 1996 to 1999, 58 children under age 5 drowned in 5-gallon buckets. Always store them upside down and store ones containing liquid with the covers securely snapped.

According to Parents for Window Blind Safety, 599 children have been seriously injured or killed in the United States since 1986 after becoming entangled in looped window treatment cords. For more information, visit pfwbs.org or cpsc.gov.

Working up high

If you have to get up on your roof to do a repair or installation, always install roof brackets and wear a roof harness.

Asbestos

Texture sprayed on ceilings before 1978, adhesives and tiles for vinyl and asphalt floors before 1980, and vermiculite insulation (with gray granules) all may contain asbestos. Other building materials, made between 1940 and 1980, could also contain asbestos. If you suspect that materials you're removing or working around contain asbestos, contact your health department or visit epa.gov/asbestos for information.

➤ **For additional information about home safety, visit mysafehome.org.**
This site offers helpful information about dozens of home safety issues.

Contents

Using Tools

Jigsaws

A jigsaw is an essential power tool for beginning DIYers because it's less intimidating than its cousin the circular saw and it's very versatile. Lots of basic projects require nothing more than a drill and a jigsaw. But DIY veterans need a jigsaw too, no matter how many other tools they own.

A jigsaw excels at cutting curves in lumber and sheet goods of every type, but can also be used to make straight cuts. Compared to a circular saw, it's quieter, lighter and—because the blade moves in a more "relaxed" up-and-down motion—safer and more user friendly. With the right blade, it can be used to cut metal, plastic pipe and tile.

Things to know:

➤ The narrower the blade, the tighter the curve it can cut. The more teeth per inch (TPI), the smoother the cut.

➤ When making a cut in the center of a board or panel, drill a 3/4-in. starter hole, insert the blade, and then proceed.

➤ For best results, cut slightly outside your cut line. Then you can use a power or hand sander for final shaping.

Get the right jigsaw for you

Some jigsaws have handles; some don't. Many pros like the no-handle "barrel-grip" style, because feel they have better control with their hands closer to the action. Folks with smaller hands often complain about the barrel being too large to grab.

OSCILLATING CONTROL

TOOL-FREE BLADE CHANGE

BASE PLATE BEVEL LEVEL

PORTER CABLE.

A blade for every occasion

There are a couple of basic things to know about jigsaw blades: The larger the teeth, the more aggressive and rougher the cut. And the narrower the blade, the tighter the turns it can make.

Match the type of blade with the material you're cutting—don't use a wood blade to cut metal. Most manufacturers have taken the guesswork out of blade selection—the description of the blade and what it does is usually written on the blade itself. Buy a combo pack and you'll be ready for most jobs.

FIBER CEMENT

DOUBLE-SIDED

CERAMIC

FLUSH-CUT

pro tips!

➤ Pushing as hard as you can on the jigsaw doesn't necessarily make it cut faster; sometimes the exact opposite is true. And pushing too hard into a curve can cause you to veer off your line, burn the material or break a blade. Ease off on the pressure until the jigsaw cuts smoothly with little vibration.

Make relief cuts for sharp turns

There's a limit on how sharp a curve a jigsaw can cut, and that depends on the blade—the narrower the blade, the sharper the turns it can make. If you try to force the blade into a turn tighter than it's capable of, you'll either veer off your line or break the blade.

If you're not sure about a particular shape, mark it out on a scrap and practice on that. If you have a curve you know is too tight, make relief cuts. The sharper the curve, the more relief cuts you'll need. And be sure you don't cut past your line. Play it safe and leave at least a blade's width of material between the relief cut and your pencil mark.

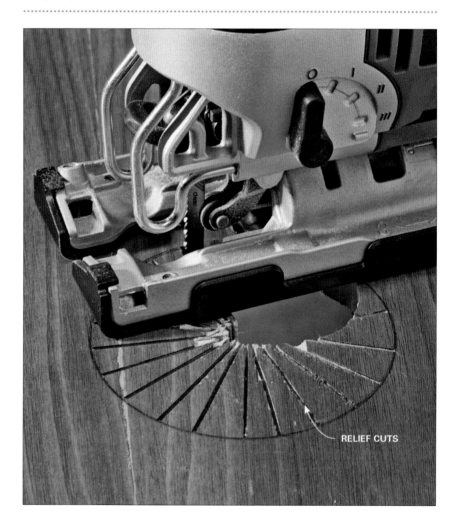

RELIEF CUTS

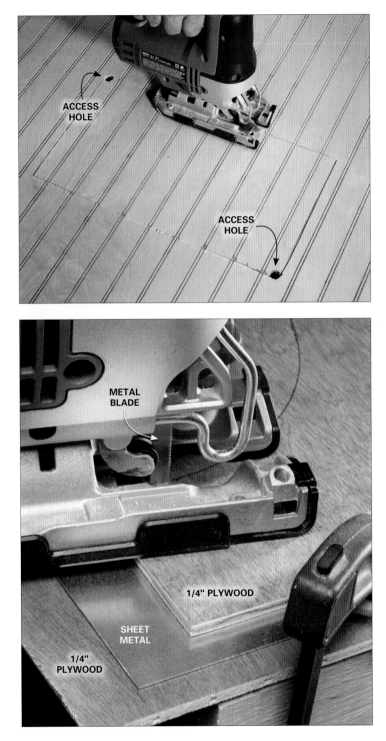

Drill access holes

If you need to cut out a hole in the center of the work surface, drill a hole slightly bigger than your jigsaw blade in two opposite corners. That way, you can make four neat cuts starting from the two holes.

ACCESS HOLE

ACCESS HOLE

Make a metal sandwich

Jigsaws are great at cutting sheet metal, but it's difficult to clamp the material down so the saw blade doesn't rattle the material up and down instead of cutting through it. One way to solve this problem is to sandwich the metal between two sheets of 1/4-in. plywood. Once the plywood is clamped down, the metal has nowhere to go, so you get a fast, easy, clean cut.

METAL BLADE

1/4" PLYWOOD

SHEET METAL

1/4" PLYWOOD

Cut with the "good" side down

Most jigsaw blades cut on the upstroke, so chips and splinters occur mostly on the top of the wood. If you value one side of a board more than the other, make sure you keep the good side face down, and mark and cut the less important side. You can buy "reverse cut" or "down cut" blades that do cut on the downstroke. These blades are used when you want as little tear-out on the top surface as possible. Cutting out a sink hole in a laminate countertop is one common use for reverse-cut blades.

TEAR-OUT

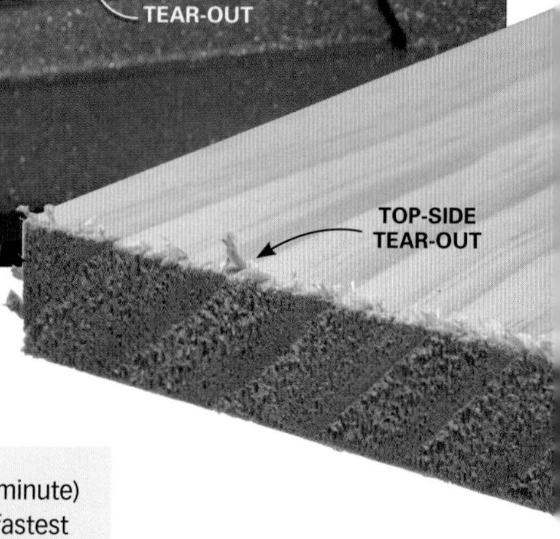

TOP-SIDE TEAR-OUT

pro tips!

➤ Typically, there's an SPM (strokes per minute) "sweet spot" where the jigsaw cuts the fastest and cleanest and with the least vibration. Try different speeds by changing pressure on the trigger. Once you find the best speed, set the adjustable speed dial so you can pull the trigger all the way while maintaining the desired SPM.

Cut anything

The main mission of a jigsaw is to cut curves in wood, and it's easy to overlook its other abilities. Instead of slaving away with your hacksaw, grab your jigsaw to quickly cut steel, copper or any metal. You can also cut plastics and tougher stuff like ceramic tile and fiber cement siding. The key to success is to match the blade to the material.

Protect the work surface

When making a cut, firmly hold down the saw to keep the blade from chattering, and even then, it may vibrate a bit. The combination of downward force and vibration is tough on the work surface. Reduce damage by applying a layer or two of masking tape to the base of the jigsaw. Remove the tape when you're done so it doesn't leave a sticky residue on the base.

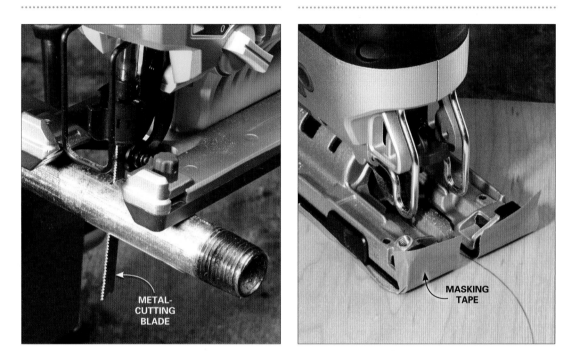

METAL-
CUTTING
BLADE

MASKING
TAPE

pro tips!

➤ Be sure the blade is up to speed before you start your cut. If you start the saw with the blade touching your material, it can grab hold and rattle the material, possibly damaging it. And let the saw come to a complete stop when you pull it from the material mid-cut. If you don't, you might experience the dreaded "woodpecker effect," when a moving blade bounces off the surface, leaving behind pockmarks and a bent blade.

Circular saws

What a hammer is to hand tools, a circular saw is to power tools; it's a must-have tool for DIYers. It shines when it comes to cutting 2x4s and other boards to length and is unequalled when it comes to cutting plywood and paneling. The standard 7-1/4-in. circular saw can cut material up to 2 in. thick and can make angled cuts up to 45 degrees. With the right blade, it can even be used to cut metal, concrete and nail-embedded lumber. For occasional use, a small cordless circular saw will suffice.

➤ Always wear hearing and eye protection.

➤ Keep the base plate (aka shoe) resting firmly on your workpiece as you cut.

➤ Position your board so the cutoff can drop away freely. In the case of plywood, make sure the piece you're cutting is well supported so it doesn't "pinch" or bind the blade.

Get the right saw for you

When shopping for a circular saw, consider corded (more powerful) vs. cordless (more convenient), weight and balance, steel shoe (less expensive) vs. aluminum shoe (more durable) and extras such as an integrated work light and easy adjustments.

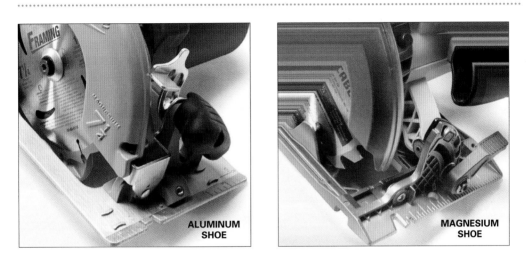

ALUMINUM SHOE

MAGNESIUM SHOE

Aluminum or magnesium shoe Steel shoes are common on less expensive saws, and they have a few downsides. First, they can bend if you drop the saw. And a bent shoe can cause your saw to cut poorly. Also, the rolled edge on a steel shoe can be a problem if you're using a thin straightedge like a rafter square for a saw guide. The saw can slip over the top of the guide and ruin the cut. We prefer aluminum or magnesium shoes with crisp, square edges. The more expensive saws in this group all have excellent shoes.

Easy depth adjustment

Changing the depth of cut on a circular saw requires you to loosen a lever and move the shoe up or down. There are two depth-adjusting features worth comparing in this group of saws. First, some saws have what we're calling an "outboard" lever; that is, the lever is located to the left of the handle where it's more accessible. We like this feature. Also, while most of the saws have some type of cutting-depth scale, the Bosch, Craftsman, Makita, Ridgid and Skil saws have exceptional scales that are easy to read. Bosch has gone one step further and included detents at common depth settings, making it quick and easy to go from cutting a 2x4 to cutting 1/2-in. plywood while maintaining the perfect blade depth.

DEPTH ADJUSTMENT LEVER

Accurate marks

To get an accurate cut with a circular saw, you have to start with an accurate mark. Stretch out your tape measure, place your pencil at the correct measurement and make two marks that form a "V," with the tip of the "V" pointing at the exact measurement. A "V" is more accurate than a single line, which can stray slightly to the right or left and throw off your cut mark.

SCRAP SIDE
OF BOARD

"V" MARK

Light up the cut

A perfect cutting line won't do you any good if you can't see it. So before you start cutting, take two seconds to check the lighting. Even in the best-lit workshops or the sunny outdoors, you or your circular saw can cast shadows that make it hard to see your cutting mark. Change the angle of the board or reposition your work light so the line won't disappear into the shadows as you cut.

CAUTION

What do earmuffs, safety glasses and dust masks have to do with cutting accurately with a circular saw? Well, it's tough to watch the cutting line with your eyes squinting and blinking through a storm of sawdust. And protection against noise, dust and splinters will make you more comfortable and more patient—and less likely to make a sloppy, rushed cut.

Shoulder the cord

On most corded circular saws, the electrical plug will snag on the edge of plywood, and that will throw off your cut. To prevent snags, drape the cord over your shoulder. Eliminate this problem completely by using a cordless saw.

Watch the blade, not the guides

Every circular saw has notches or marks on the front of the shoe to indicate where the blade is going to cut. Unfortunately, they get covered with sawdust or the whole thing gets bent out of whack, which throws off the guide. Watch the actual blade and line as you cut. All it takes is a light puff of air every few seconds to clear the sawdust.

Score a clean cut

Circular saws usually splinter the wood that's facing up and cut cleanly on the side that's facing down. So when you're cutting, always position the material "good side down." Pushing your circular saw more slowly than normal also helps reduce splintering.

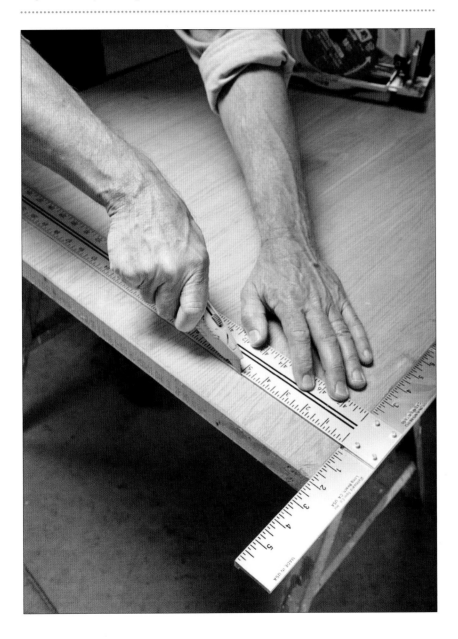

Rotary tools

This tool, often referred to by the brand name Dremel, operates like a high-speed mini-drill, but oddly enough is rarely used as a drill. The chuck (or collet) can grasp a variety of bits that can be used for carving, sanding, engraving and polishing. Cordless versions are adequate for light use and when pursuing small-scale hobby work. Accessories ranging from flexible shafts to jigsaw attachments are available. Always wear safety glasses when using a rotary tool. DIYers may find the tool particularly useful for:

➤ Removing burrs from pipes or other metals after cutting.

➤ Engraving names and initials on tools and other frequently "borrowed" items.

➤ Removing finishes or sanding wood in hard-to-access places.

Cut stubborn parts

A rotary tool is often the best solution when corrosion has caused metal parts to get stuck. With a rotary tool, either slice off the stubborn metal part, or cut slits in it so you can break it off.

ROTARY
TOOL

Vacuum-powered rotary tool

This Dremel rotary tool has no motor and is powered solely by the suction of a vacuum! If you want to keep dust to a minimum on sanding projects, this is the tool for you.

Fix a door that doesn't latch

Instead of moving the strike plate, simply slightly enlarge the latch opening in the strike plate. A rotary tool does this quickly and easily. Use a carbide-cutting bit specifically designed for metal cutting. Judge the part of the strike plate that needs grinding by testing when the latch catches. If you have to push down on the doorknob, then the top of the strike plate hole needs grinding. If the door has to be pushed in, then grind the outside edge of the strike plate hole. You don't want the latch slopping around inside a huge opening, so don't grind away half the strike plate. Remove small amounts of metal and then test the door. Repeat until the door latch effortlessly catches the strike plate.

CAUTION

Grinding metal can throw sparks and fragments into the air, so wear safety glasses with side shields, or full goggles when grinding. Otherwise, use a small round file for this project.

ROTARY
TOOL

METAL-CUTTING
CARBIDE BIT

Cut holes in tile

A rotary tool is a great, safe way to cut through tile. Set the depth of the tile-cutting bit shallow to avoid hitting plumbing or wires in the wall cavity. Whenever possible, use grout lines for two sides of the hole because they're much easier to cut through. Drill starter holes in two opposite corners with a glass-and-tile drill bit.

STARTER HOLE

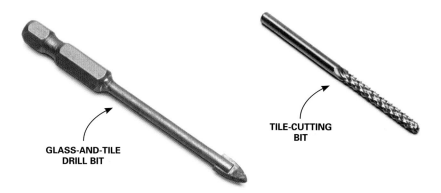

GLASS-AND-TILE DRILL BIT

TILE-CUTTING BIT

Dishwasher rack repair

Dishwasher rack tines break off or lose the protective coating at the tips and then you get rust spots on your dishes. But you can fix this with help from a rotary tool. Buy a bottle of vinyl repair paint and a package of replacement tips to match your rack from any appliance parts store or online. Cut off the rusted tips with a rotary tool and cutoff wheel. Then retip the tines (**Photo 1**). To patch a rusted area around a broken tine, first clean off the rust (**Photo 2**).

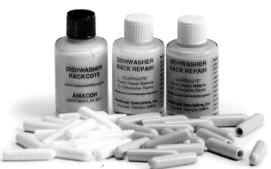

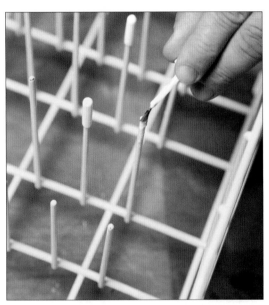

1. **Paint and new tips**. Coat the freshly cut tip with vinyl paint. Then slip a new vinyl tip over the tine.

2. **Clean the rack**. Load a wire brush into a rotary tool and zip off the old rust and vinyl. Keep brushing until you get to fresh metal. Then paint on a new coating.

Dust-sucking rotary tool

Nothing works better at cutting holes in drywall than a rotary tool. It's also true that nothing fills a room with dust faster. This RotoZip rotary tool has an integrated dust collection system that reduces airborne dust by up to 90 percent. It also works on wood, cement board and tile, among other materials.

Cut stainless steel with a grinding disc

There are many types of stainless steel, and some hard varieties are challenging to cut. For small jobs like cutting stainless steel backsplash tiles, a rotary tool fitted with an abrasive metal-cutting disc works fine.

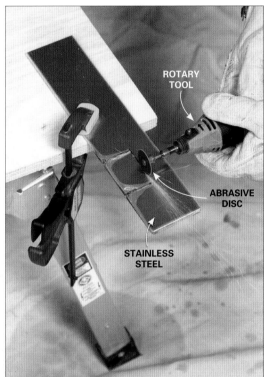

ROTARY TOOL

ABRASIVE DISC

STAINLESS STEEL

Oscillating tools

This is the Swiss Army Knife of power tools; compact, versatile and able to get into areas and perform tasks no other tool can. This barrel-shaped tool has a short vibrating shaft, to which a variety of accessories can be attached for cutting, scraping or sanding. It's often used for repairs and remodeling. Do-it-yourselfers will find it particularly useful for:

➤ Cutting off pipes and rusted bolts in tight spaces.

➤ Sanding or scraping in tight corners or spaces when refinishing furniture or floors.

➤ Removing old grout, caulk and floor adhesives when remodeling.

From hospitals to job sites

In 1968, Fein patented the oscillating "plaster cast saw," which could slice through a cast without harming the patient's skin. That medical tool evolved into the do-anything tool we know today. Fein still makes pro-grade oscillating tools, and many pros swear it's still the best choice.

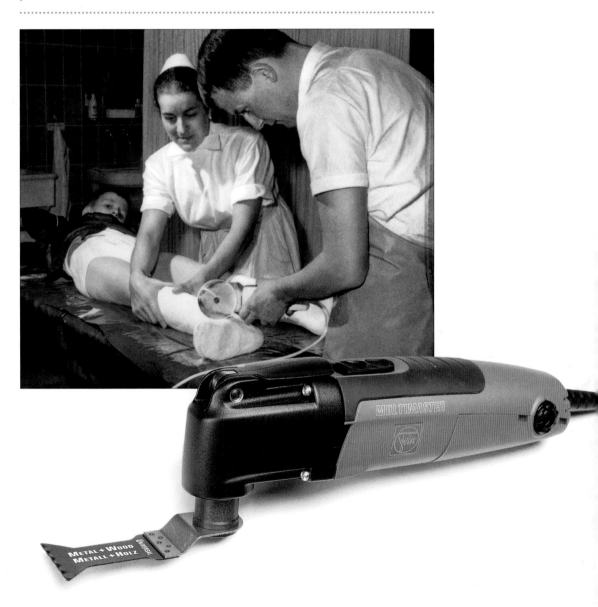

How it works

An oscillating tool works with a side-to-side movement. The oscillation is very slight (about 3 degrees) and very fast (about 20,000 strokes per minute), so it feels more like vibration. A saw blade is shown; the tool also works with scrapers and sanding pads.

Cut stubborn parts

An oscillating tool works great for cutting toilet bolts that are rusted or corroded.

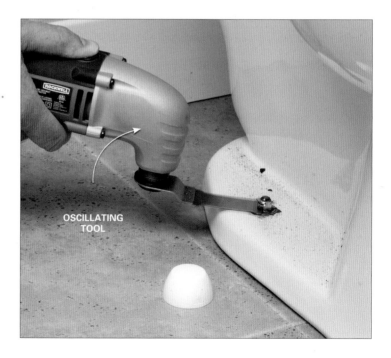

OSCILLATING TOOL

Get into tight spots

When access is tight, or you need to make a flush cut, an oscillating tool fitted with a metal-cutting blade will solve the problem. Corroded mounting nuts on toilets and faucets are easy to cut off with an oscillating tool. You can also use an oscillating tool to cut plumbing pipes, automotive bolts, nails and other metal objects in places where a larger tool wouldn't fit. Just make sure the blade is intended to cut metal.

METAL-CUTTING BLADE

OSCILLATING TOOL

pro tips!

➤ **Don't burn up the blade.** Heat kills blades. Occasionally swing the blade back and forth out of the cut to clean out dust. And don't press too hard.

Remove old caulk

Slice through the old caulk along walls and floors with an oscillating tool equipped with a flexible scraper blade. This often works better than a utility knife.

pro tips!

➤ Oscillating tools are usually sold as kits with varying assortments of accessories. Considering the high cost of blades, checking the contents of the kit is worthwhile. Don't just look at the number of pieces, though: A 30-piece kit might include 25 low-cost sanding pads.

CAUTION

Most blades sold in stores are meant for soft materials like wood and plastic. Cutting metal destroys them in a few seconds. For metal cutting, be sure to buy blades labeled "bimetal," "titanium" or just "metal."

The best way to remove grout

If you have grout that's stained or moldy, the best tool for the job is an oscillating tool fitted with a diamond blade. An oscillating tool won't damage any tiles or whip up a dust storm. You'll need at least two diamond blades, depending on the size of the job. Switch to a scraper blade for your oscillating tool to scrape away caulk at the inside corners.

pro tips!

➤ **Blades are a big expense.** Oscillating tool blades are pricey and wear out fast. Over the life of your oscillating tool, you'll probably spend more on blades than on the tool itself.

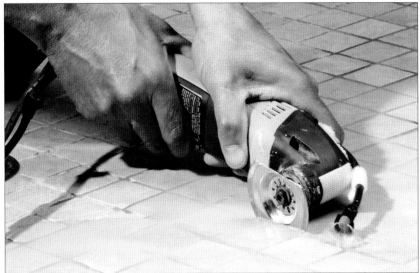

Special oscillating tool blades

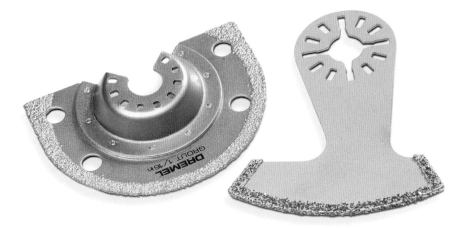

Great for grout removal. A carbide is fine for small jobs. For larger jobs, a diamond blade saves you money because it lasts two to three times as long. Both types come in 1/16-in. and 1/8-in. thicknesses to match grout widths. When you see sparks, you know that the outer edge of the blade is worn out, even though there may be plenty of grit left on the sides of the blade.

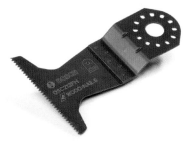

Scraper blades. These blades come in lots of styles: stiff or flexible, sharp or blunt, straight or offset. This long , thin version is good for digging caulk out of joints. The other blade works well for scraping patches of dried construction adhesive off of the floor.

Extra-wide blades. Extra-wide blades like this 2-1/2-in. version are perfect for cutting round stuff like pipe because they don't slip off a curved surface the way narrow blades do. For other jobs, narrower blades are usually best: They plunge-cut better and put less strain on the motor.

Faster flooring prep

With a scrap of flooring as a guide, an oscillating tool also makes a straight, clean cut. The only downside is the noise. (Oscillating tools are loud!) Hearing protection is a good idea.

SCRAP

A flush-cutting blade is best for undercutting doorjambs. The raised center lets the blade sit flat on a guide scrap. With a flat blade, the tool's bolt head protrudes below, so the blade can't ride over a guide.

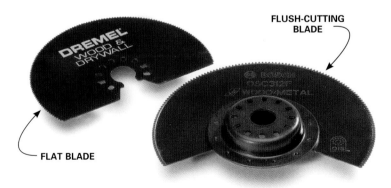

FLUSH-CUTTING BLADE

FLAT BLADE

Brad nailers

A brad nailer (aka a trim nailer) is a "gun" used for driving small finish nails ranging in length from 1/2 inch to 2 inches; it can be cordless, electric or pneumatic. If you're installing trim, building furniture, assembling picture frames or tackling any other project that requires more than a few dozen nails, a brad nailer is well worth the investment. They not only increase speed, but since they drive nails in a single pop and eliminate the jarring of hammering, they also improve accuracy.

➤ Always wear sight and hearing protection. Keep safety in the forefront.

➤ Keep your free hand and your body out of the projected path of nails.

➤ Press the nosepiece, which contains a small "safety" tongue that must be depressed, firmly against the workpiece before pulling the trigger.

The nails

Brad nailers are categorized by the thickness or "gauge" of the nails they shoot: The bigger the gauge number, the smaller the nail (seems backward, doesn't it?). Nailers that shoot the biggest nails, 15 and 16 gauge, are usually called "finish nailers." Midsize 18-gauge nailers are called "brad nailers." The smallest nailer, the 23-gauge, is usually called a "pinner" or "micro pinner."

23-GAUGE

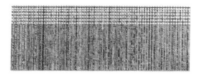

18-GAUGE

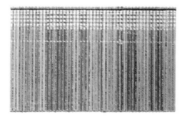

16-GAUGE

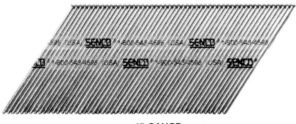

15-GAUGE

The basics

Bare tool or kit? Most cordless brad nailers are available as kits containing a battery and charger. If you own other battery-powered tools, you'll save money if you can find a brad nailer that uses the same battery. Otherwise, the kits are usually a better deal.

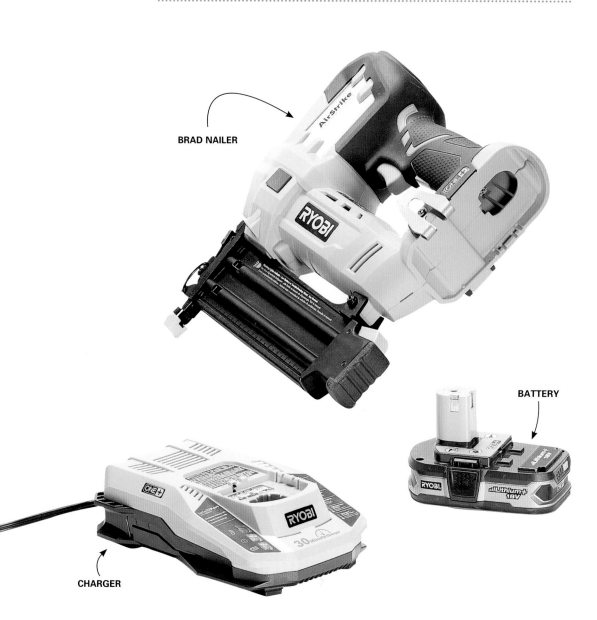

BRAD NAILER

BATTERY

CHARGER

Tool weight matters

If you're installing crown molding overhead, a few pounds could make
the difference between aching shoulders and a pain-free job.

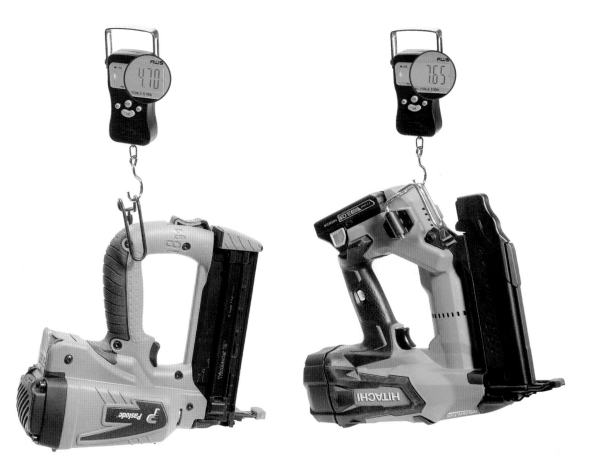

Use a brad nailer for perfect mitered corners

It's hard to beat a brad nailer for perfect miters, especially if you're not skilled with a hammer. Brad nailers allow you to hold the moldings in perfect alignment while you pin them in place. If you can afford only one nailer, buy one that shoots thin 18-gauge nails up to 2 in. long. Fifteen- and 16-gauge nailers are good where more strength is needed, such as for nailing door jambs, but the thicker brads make larger, more conspicuous holes and can crack thin moldings. Use shorter brads to nail the molding to the jamb, and long brads along the outside edges.

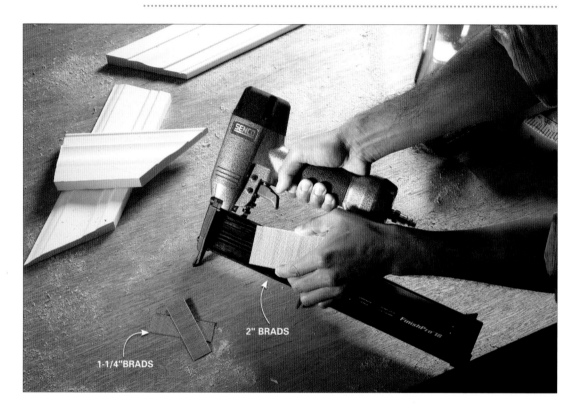

2" BRADS

1-1/4"BRADS

PIN THE MITER

1. In a perfect world, you could nail the trim flat to the wall and the miter would look great. But in reality, minor variations in level between the jamb and the wall often interfere. To solve this problem, start by pinning the inside edge of the trim, making sure the miter joint is pressed tight together. Then, while the miter is still tight, drive a pair of brads through the outside corners at opposite angles to pin it.

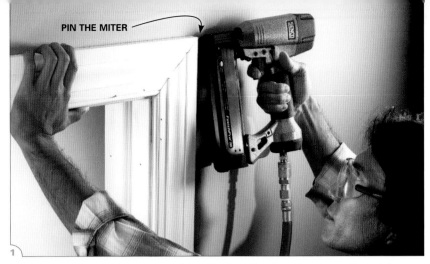

THIN SHIM

2. If there's a slight gap between the molding and the wall, don't press the trim tight to the wall and nail it; the miter joint might open up. Instead, slip a thin shim between the molding and the wall. Then nail the outside edge of the trim. If the gap and shim are visible, fill the crack with caulk before painting.

Chapter 2

DIY Products and Materials

Plywood

Plywood, normally available in 4- x 8-ft. sheets, is made of thin plies of wood that have been stacked in layers and then pressed and glued together. The result is a large, durable "slab of wood" that can be cut, shaped and assembled in literally thousands of ways. Why so many piles of the stuff in the home center? It comes in thicknesses ranging from 1/8 in. to 3/4 in. Some plywood is designated for indoor use, some is for outdoor use. And plywood comes in a variety of grades. Some is attractive enough for building cabinets, other plywood is for structural uses like roof and floor sheathing.

➤ Most home centers will give you a few free cuts, meaning less cutting for you (and easier hauling home).

➤ Oriented strand board (OSB) is similar to plywood, but is made of wood chips rather than wood plies. It's generally cheaper and usually used in structural situations.

➤ Solidly support large sheets of plywood on scrap 2x4s while cutting.

pro tips!

- **Check for flatness.** Don't expect perfection—you probably won't find it. Just try to find the best of the pile.

- **Inspect the edges.** Look closely at the core veneers on the edge of the sheet. They should be straight and of uniform thickness and have few, if any, voids. If you see a lot of voids and overlapping core veneers along the edge, there will be more throughout the sheet that won't be visible until you cut it. Overlapping veneers cause undulations that aren't visible until after you've applied a finish.

VOID

- **Bring a friend.** Plywood in 4 x 8-ft. sheets is heavy and unwieldy. Unstacking, inspecting, restacking, loading and unloading are much easier with an extra set of hands.

- **Beware of birch.** Any species accepts a clear finish such as polyurethane just fine. But if you're planning to stain your piece, beware of birch, pine and maple. These species take stain very unevenly and can end up looking blotchy. If you're set on one of these species, use prestain conditioner, which helps them take stain much more evenly. Even better, look at samples of different species with a clear finish and see if there's one that has the color you like without stain.

- **Don't have plywood delivered.** If you have a way to haul sheets of plywood yourself, do it. The person pulling sheets for delivery isn't going to hand-select the nicest sheets for you. If delivery is your only option, inspect the sheets before the delivery truck leaves and reject any that are damaged or unusable. You may not have the option of rejecting a sheet because you don't like the grain pattern.

- **Using paint? Choose MDF or birch.** For projects You're going to paint, choose MDF (medium-density fiberboard) or birch. B-grade birch or lower is fine. Sometimes, you'll even see plywood classified as "paint grade." Birch is close-grained with a smooth texture that doesn't show through paint. With an open-grained species like oak, the grain is visible under paint. MDF, of course, has no grain pattern, making it a good choice for painted projects. But for structural parts, use birch veneer. For tips on building with MDF, search for "MDF" at familyhandyman.com.

Core options

The materials used to make plywood's inner core affect several important characteristics: weight, strength, rigidity, stability, flatness, screw-holding capability, consistency of thickness, and evenness of the veneer.

Veneer core is made up of many layers of hardwood bonded together. The layers are assembled with alternating grain direction, called crossbanding. This makes a strong, rigid, lightweight sheet with excellent screw-holding capability.

MDF core has a few advantages over veneer core. The thickness is more consistent, and MDF gives a smooth, even surface for the face veneer. It's also more stable and it's typically flatter. However, MDF core isn't as strong as veneer core, it doesn't hold fasteners as well and it's heavy.

Particleboard core is the least expensive option. Like MDF core, it's flat and stable with consistent thickness. But particleboard core is a bit worse in the screw-holding category.

Combination core weds the best attributes of MDF core and veneer core. The center cores are crossbanded hardwood, providing strength, light weight and screw-holding capability. The outer cores are MDF, giving a flat, uniform surface for the face veneers. However, combination core is a compromise: It doesn't have the screw-holding capability and rigidity of veneer core, or the flatness and stability of MDF core.

Lumber core consists of edge-glued strips of wood, usually basswood. On both sides of the core, there's a crossbanded veneer, then the face veneer. Like veneer core, it has excellent screw-holding capability, strength and rigidity. But it's considerably more expensive and harder to find than veneer core. It's a good choice for long shelves.

Baltic birch and AplePly are top-notch veneer core plywoods, which you'll only find at a lumberyard. Their 1/16-in.-thick core veneers offer better stability than typical plywood. The raw edge is attractive when finished and often used as a design element.

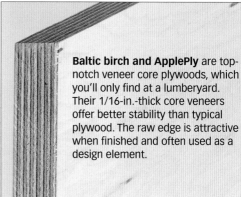

Plywood grades

Hardwood veneer plywood has a front and a back face and is graded by the quality of each face. The front face is graded using a letter (A–D), with A being the best. The back face is graded using a number (1–4), with 1 being the best.

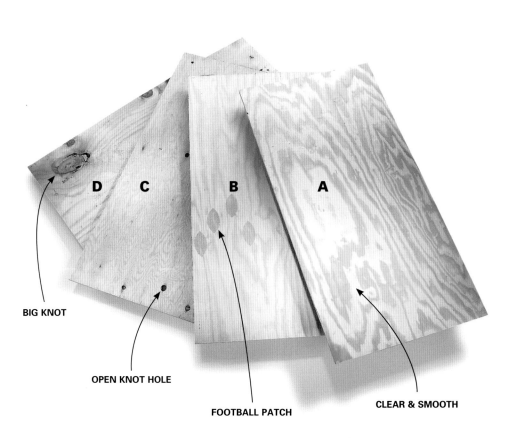

D   C   B   A

BIG KNOT

OPEN KNOT HOLE

FOOTBALL PATCH

CLEAR & SMOOTH

How veneer is cut

The way the veneer was sliced from the log determines its look. The more common cuts—rotary and plain—are also the least expensive. Quarter-sawn and rift-sawn are more labor intensive to cut and are considered more attractive by most people.

 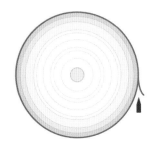

ROTARY-CUT veneer is peeled from the log like paper towels from a roll. It produces a wide, "loud" grain pattern.

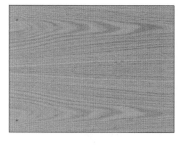 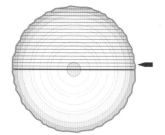

PLAIN-SLICING produces a repeating pattern, typically showing large "cathedrals" in the grain.

 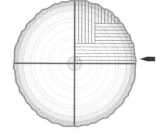

RIFT-SAWING produces veneer with tight, straight lines.

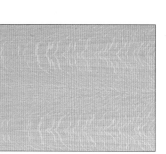 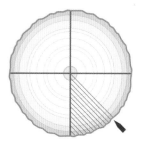

QUARTER-SAWING produces veneer with the same tight, straight lines as rift-sawing but includes the signature "ray flecks."

Plywood handling tips

You can easily move 4- x 8-ft. sheets of plywood by yourself with this carrier. It's a 30-in.-long x 12-in.-wide piece of 1/2-in. plywood with a carrying hook at the end. Make the hook by attaching a 2-in. and a 4-in. piece of 3/4-in. plywood with glue and screws. Cut a handle slot 2 in. down from the other end.

This carrier is designed for people of average height. If you're on the short side, nest your underarm over a sheet of plywood, mark your hand position on the sheet and lengthen the carrier accordingly.

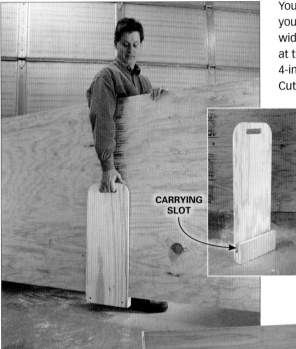

CARRYING SLOT

TOWEL

Carrying a 4x8 sheet of plywood or other building material by yourself can be difficult. To make it easier, grab a tie-down strap and a towel. Set the plywood on its long edge and attach one tie-down hook at each end. Wrap the towel around the middle of the strap and sling it over your shoulder. Using your free arm to steady the plywood, haul away the sheet of plywood.

Melamine

Melamine is the common name for particleboard that's coated with a thin layer of plastic finish. The melamine finish is similar to the plastic laminate on countertops, but it's not as thick. It's durable enough to withstand moderate abuse and can usually be cleaned using a damp rag. You can buy 4- x 8-ft. panels of melamine-coated particleboard for building your own furniture or storage units, but beware —the stuff is heavy! The advantages of building with a melamine-coated product are its durable finish and its relatively low cost. But it can be frustrating to work with. The particleboard can be hard to fasten, and the brittle finish is tricky to cut.

➤ Cut "good side down" to avoid chipping on the visible side.

➤ Use a fine-tooth blade for cleanest cuts.

➤ Iron-on edging is available to cover and protect exposed edges.

1. **Buy a special blade.** The melamine finish chips easily when cut, especially if you're using an ordinary saw blade. But you can largely avoid chipping by investing in a special blade that's designed to cut plastic materials. The teeth on these blades are less angled, which helps prevent chipping. If you can't justify spending more for a special blade, you can still get good results with a less expensive blade that has at least 40 carbide teeth. Also, check out the chip-free cutting technique in Tip 4, p. 51.

2. **Order the color you want.** You'll typically find white melamine products at home centers, but many colors are available. Depending on the brand, you'll find 10 to 20 or more colors available for special order. Check with your local lumberyard or home center for your options.

pro tips!

➤ Look around and you'll find melamine furniture, melamine shelves, melamine wall panels, and even melamine slatwall. It's usually labeled as melamine, but you may also see terms such as thermally fused laminate or simply prefinished panels or prefinished shelves. You can buy 4- x 8-ft. sheets of melamine in 1/8-, 1/4-, 1/2-, 5/8- and 3/4-in. thicknesses and melamine shelves in various lengths and widths. Home centers may only stock 1/4-in. and 3/4-in. thicknesses.

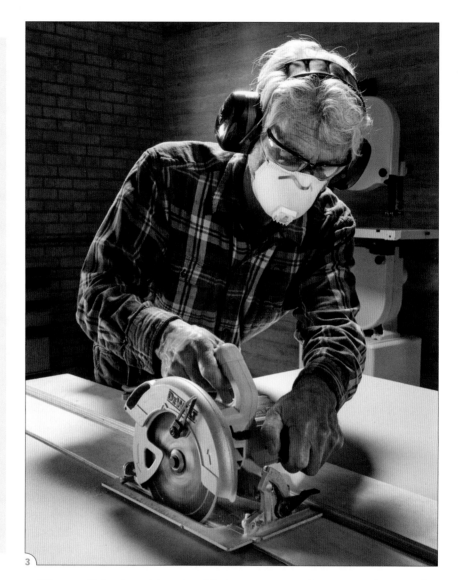

3

3. **Wear safety gear.** You should always wear safety gear when you're using power tools. There are particular safety concerns when you're working with melamine. For starters, the plastic finish tends to chip off as it's cut. The chips are as sharp as glass, creating a real hazard for your eyes. Safety glasses are a must. The fine dust created by cutting the fiber core is bad for your lungs. If possible, cut outdoors. Indoors or out, wear a dust mask. Wear gloves when you're handling large sheets of melamine. The edges can be razor sharp. And don't forget hearing protection.

SHALLOW
SAW KERF

4

4. **Cut without chipping.** Making a scoring cut before the final one
will result in a chip-free edge. First, use a straightedge as a saw
guide. Without the straightedge, the saw might wobble slightly
as you cut, and this twisting will contribute to chipping. Clamp
your straightedge guide in position and set the saw to cut 1/8 in.
deep. Run your saw along the straightedge and cut a groove in
the melamine panel. This shallow cut shouldn't produce any chipping. Now reset the saw so the blade extends about 1/2 in. past
the bottom side of the panel and make another pass. The resulting
cut will be perfectly chip-free on both sides. You can use the same
technique on a table saw. Make one shallow cut. Then run the panel
through the saw a second time to complete the cut. If only one side
of the panel will be visible in the finished project, you don't need to
use this technique because chipping occurs only on the side where
the saw blade teeth exit. Just make sure to place the "show" side
down if you're cutting with a circular saw and up when you're using
a table saw.

5. **Pin panels, then add screws.** The melamine finish is slippery, making it difficult to hold the panels in alignment while you drill pilot holes for the screws. Solve this problem by first pinning the panels together using an 18-gauge brad nailer (see p. 34). The small holes left by the brads are nearly invisible, and you'll save yourself a lot of time and frustration.

6. **Drill and countersink screws.** Particleboard, whether it has a melamine finish or not, doesn't hold screws as well as solid lumber or plywood. Plus, it tends to split if you drive screws without drilling first. The key to fastening melamine with screws is to drill pilot holes for the screws and countersinks* for the screw heads. A combination bit that drills and countersinks in one operation saves time. Choose a countersink bit that's labeled for use with No. 8 screws.

COUNTERSINK BIT

*Countersink: A recess in which a screwhead can be set flush with or below the surface.

7. **Prevent splitting**. Melamine's particleboard core is brittle and can split if you drive screws too close to the edge. Prevent this by positioning screws at least 2 in. from the edge of panels when possible. Drilling a pilot hole also helps prevent splitting (see Tip 6).

8. **Hide screw heads**. To conceal screw heads, you have a couple of options. You can buy plastic caps that snap onto or over your screw heads. These work fine but leave a protruding cap. The other option is to cover the screw with FastCap self-sticking plastic screw covers These are available at some retailers, online or directly from FastCap. Go to fastcap.com to see the huge variety of sizes and colors.

pro tips!

➤ **Buy shelving with edges finished.** Shelving with finished edges is readily available at home centers and hardware stores. The only drawback is that the color selection may be limited.

Caulk (interior and exterior)

Caulk—sold in barrel-shaped tubes with a snout emerging from one end—is used to fill small cracks between building materials. Outside it can be used to fill gaps around siding, windows, doors, corner boards, flashings and gutters. Inside it's commonly used to seal gaps around sinks and bathtubs, and spaces between moldings and trim before painting.

It's dispensed via a caulk gun with a plunger that pushes the caulk out through the nozzle. For super-small jobs, you can buy toothpaste-size tubes of caulk. Keep in mind:

➤ The best tool for smoothing caulk after it's applied is your finger.

➤ Caulks are available in a limited range of colors; some are paintable, others aren't. Buy accordingly.

➤ The label will tell you whether it's intended for indoor or outdoor use and also give you a rough idea of its longevity.

Exterior siding and trim: Hybrid or polyurethane. On your home's exterior, high-quality caulk is critical—it locks out water, protecting your home against rot and peeling paint. Although some inexpensive acrylic latex caulks are rated for exterior use, we recommend hybrid caulks because they offer better adhesion and flexibility.

1. **Acrylic latex.** caulks are the easiest to apply and smooth out. They're also the only sealants that clean up with water. Look for versions labeled "siliconized" or "plus silicone." Adding silicone to acrylic latex improves adhesion and flexibility.

2. **Polyurethane.** caulks are generally tougher than other sealants, making them a good choice for driveways and other areas that take a beating. But their gooey consistency makes them hard to work with. Check the label before painting; you may have to wait several days.

3. **Solvent-based.** caulks are great for roofing because they don't degrade in direct sunlight and can be applied to wet surfaces. But they're gooey and hard to apply neatly.

4. **Hybrid.** caulks combine silicone and polyurethane for top-notch adhesion, flexibility and longevity. They're easier to apply neatly than polyurethane, but not as easy as acrylic latex. Cost is a clue: High-quality hybrids are usually the most expensive caulks on the shelf.

pro tips!

➤ **Expensive caulk is worth it.** The most common reason for using caulk, whether indoors or out, is to prevent water penetration—and serious damage. That's why spending an extra five bucks on high-quality caulk is usually smart.

Interior painting

This is the one project for which it doesn't make sense to spend a lot of money. For just a couple bucks, you can find an acrylic latex caulk that dries fast, is easy to work with, easy to clean up and can handle a little movement. If you have a large recurring crack in a wall corner or in a crown molding joint, choose a product with better flexibility such as a hybrid formula.

Kitchen and bath

Caulk in kitchens and bathrooms is often visible, so choosing a product that's easy to apply neatly is important. It also needs to be waterproof, and mold and mildew resistant. Choose a product labeled with those traits. Acrylic latex kitchen and bath caulks are the easiest to work with, but hybrids generally have a longer life span.

pro tips!

➤ **What about silicone?** Years ago, silicone caulk was a good choice for many jobs. Today, there are better options for almost every situation. So why is silicone still so popular? Here's what one manufacturer of caulks (including silicone) told us: "Silicone is what our customers saw their fathers use. It's what they're familiar with."

Concrete and masonry

A specialty caulk specially formulated for concrete and masonry will outperform general-purpose products. Most concrete and masonry sealants are polyurethane or hybrid formulas. Some concrete and masonry caulks are self-leveling and can be used only on level surfaces.

Roofing

Any caulk that lives on a roof is going to get hammered by the elements. It needs to be able to survive extreme exposure to sunlight and temperature variations yet remain flexible. Solvent-based sealants work best in these conditions.

Gutters

It's no surprise that a product designed to seal gutters needs to be 100-percent waterproof. But it also needs to be tough enough to handle the abrasion from debris and ice in cold climates. Most gutter sealants do a good job on metal, but not all will adhere to plastic gutters. Be sure to check the label and look for a hybrid or solvent-based product.

Concrete

"Quick mix" or "ready mix" concrete is available in 60- and 80-pound bags. Each bag contains a blend of cement, sand and gravel that requires only the addition of water before use. It can be used to install fence or mailbox posts, create footings for deck posts and for pouring small slabs. Once in place, it sets up or hardens in a few hours and is ready for use in a day or two. Mixing it correctly is the key to a successful job. Too much water will result in weak concrete, too little and the particles won't bind together. Place the bag in a wheelbarrow and dump out the contents. Using a bucket, slowly add water while turning the mixture over with a shovel or "raking it" back and forth with a hoe. Each bag will require 2 to 3 quarts of water. A few tips:

➤ Rinse off your wheelbarrow and tools ASAP; hardened concrete is a bear to remove.

➤ Ready-mix concrete serves a different role than the bags of cement, mortar and other materials sitting next to it in the home center. Buy the right stuff.

➤ Wear gloves, eye and respiratory protection when handling concrete; some of the ingredients are caustic.

Concrete recipe

Aside from cement, concrete contains sand and stones. Those stones, or "aggregate," are a carefully measured mix of various sizes. Small stones fill in the gaps between larger ones, and sand fills in between them. Cement is the glue that holds it all together.

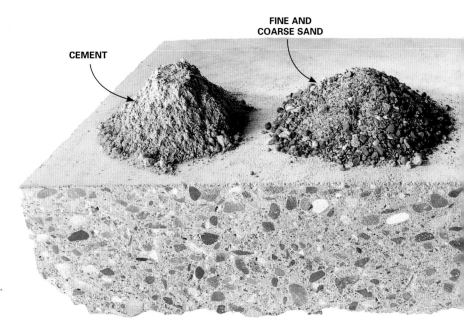

CEMENT

FINE AND COARSE SAND

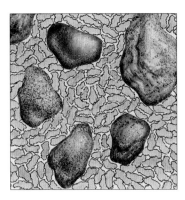

Water makes concrete "work"

Cement is mostly limestone that's been ground up and superheated. Adding water causes a chemical reaction; microscopic crystals develop, grow and interlock, binding the aggregate together and forming a rock-hard mass.

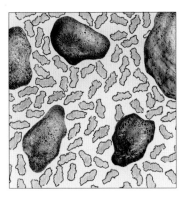

Too much water makes it weak

It's tempting to add extra water to make concrete easier to work with or to soften concrete that has begun to harden. But don't do it. With too much water, cement crystals develop too far apart, leaving concrete weak and porous.

pro tips!

➤ **It's *not* "cement."** Most people say "cement" and "concrete" interchangeably. But they're not the same thing. Cement is just one of the ingredients in concrete, and if you ask for cement at the lumberyard, you might get a bag of Portland cement, which is not what you want.

➤ **Concrete doesn't "dry."** Concrete hardens while it's wet—not as it dries. If, for example, you throw a bag of concrete mix into a bathtub full of water, it will harden underwater (but we really don't recommend you do that).

FLOAT

DARBY

AGGREGATE

WEAK, POROUS SURFACE

PLASTIC SHEET

Keep it wet longer to make it stronger

Concrete will continue to harden until it dries out completely. That's why pros often use blankets, plastic sheets or spray-on coatings to retain moisture. Since most of the strength gain takes place in the first few days, experts often recommend a "wet cure" of three to seven days. Typically, concrete is considered fully cured after 28 days.

Don't overwork it

To finish the surface, concrete is first "floated" with a float or a darby. This pushes the aggregate down and pulls fine sand and cement to the surface—just what you need to form a smooth, troweled finish or a rough-broomed finish later. But limit float work to two or three passes. Too much floating leaves a topping of watery cement. And that means a weak, porous surface. Too much troweling causes the same problems.

Simple safety

Cement is caustic. So it can cause anything from dry skin to nasty burns that require medical attention. Wear gloves and protect your eyes. Concrete dust is bad for your lungs. So strap on a respirator while mixing or cutting it.

GROOVER

CONTROL
JOINT

trivia

➤ **Beyond concrete:** Portland cement is also the key ingredient in other building materials such as mortar, stucco and tile grout.

Allow for cracks

Concrete shrinks as it cures, which causes shrinkage cracks. Settling and frost heaves also lead to cracks. Instead of risking random, meandering cracks, provide "control joints" for straight, invisible cracks to occur. You can plow control joints into fresh concrete with a groover (as shown here) or use a saw when the concrete is partially cured. On sidewalks, control joints are needed every 4 to 5 ft. On wide slabs like driveways, place them 10 to 12 ft. apart.

pro tips!

➤ **A little thicker is a lot stronger.** A 4-in.-thick sidewalk is fine. But for driveways or slabs that will bear heavy loads, go for at least 5 in. That extra inch provides about 50 percent more strength but adds only a few hundred bucks to the cost.

Speedy concrete

By adding an "accelerator" to the mix, manufacturers produce bagged concrete that hardens in an hour or less. That's great for small jobs but risky for big jobs that require ample finishing time.

trivia

➤ **Convenient concrete:** In the 1930s, bagged concrete mix hit the market. Before that, folks had to mix up cement, sand and aggregate themselves.

How to mix bagged concrete

For most small jobs around the home, bagged concrete mix is the most convenient and least expensive way to go. You can use it for fence post footings, deck footings and even small concrete pads. For jobs requiring more than about 30 bags, consider ordering "ready-mix" concrete from a truck instead.

1. Set the bag of concrete mix in one end of the wheelbarrow and slice it open with your hoe. Dump the mix from the bag and pull out the paper bag.

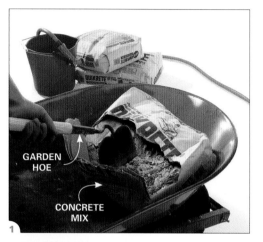

GARDEN HOE

CONCRETE MIX

2. Fill a bucket with the specific amount of water recommended on the bag (amount varies with bag size). For future reference, mark the water level with a permanent marker. Pour the water into the opposite end of the wheelbarrow, reserving about 4 cups to add later if needed.

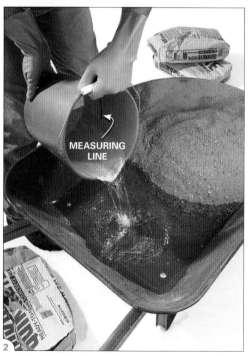

MEASURING LINE

PULL DRY MIX

TOO DRY

CRUMBLY MIX

TOO RUNNY

JUST RIGHT

SIDES STAY PUT

SHINY FLAT SPOT

3. Pull a small amount of the dry mix into the water with a hoe and mix it completely. Continue pulling and mixing until all of the powder is wetted and the mix is piled at your end of the wheelbarrow. Continue mixing by going to the other end of the wheelbarrow and pulling the mix back toward you.

4. Drag the hoe through the mix to make a trough. The mix is too dry if the sides of the trough are crumbly and the concrete falls in chunks when you disturb it. Add water one cup at a time, mixing between each addition.

5. Add more dry concrete if the mix is too wet and soupy and sags into the trench.

6. The mix is just right when the sides of the trough stand and the ingredients are thoroughly wetted. A hoe patted against the concrete will leave a slightly shiny surface.

7. Scrub the wheelbarrow and tools with a stiff-bristle brush before the concrete starts to harden. Rinse well.

pro tips!

➤ It's tempting to just squirt water into the dry concrete mix with a hose and mix up a soupy batch of concrete. After all, it's quicker and the runny concrete is easier to pour. The trouble is, soupy concrete is only about half as strong as a proper mix and is more likely to crack. That's why we recommend spending a little extra time measuring the water into a bucket first, and adding only as much as is needed. Even though the thicker mix is a little harder to place, it'll be worth the extra effort.

Use a sturdy wheelbarrow to mix your concrete. And make sure it's on a level surface. Brace the wheelbarrow with your knee when you're mixing from the side.

How to estimate a concrete order

Here's a brief rundown of what you need to know if your project requires more concrete than what you can mix up yourself. This example is for a 10- x 10-ft. concrete slab.

- ➤ **Amount.** Calculate the volume you need in cubic yards. Multiply the length (10 ft.) by the width (10 ft.) by the depth (.35 ft.,or 4 in.) and divide it by 27 (the number of cubic feet in a cubic yard). You get 1.3 cu. yds. Then add 10 percent to allow for spillage and slab depth variations.

- ➤ **Strength.** Call a local ready-mix company, tell the supplier what the concrete is for, and ask about the best mix (proportions of cement, gravel and sand). For a shed, the supplier will probably suggest a mix with a capacity of about 4,000 psi (pounds per square inch). If you live in a region with freeze/thaw cycles in winter, ask for 5 percent air entrainment to help the concrete withstand freeze/thaw damage.

- ➤ **Cost.** Use $160 per cubic yard as a ballpark figure, but this will vary by region. Also, they may charge a $400 minimum delivery fee and there could be additional fees for such things as Saturday delivery and small loads. Ask about these fees so you know the total bill before the truck arrives.

- ➤ **Unload time.** Ask about the normal unload time (usually 7 to 10 minutes per yard) and if there is a fee for overtime. If the truck can't reach the site, make sure you have two or three people with wheelbarrows ready to go.

Lubricants

A lubricant is a substance (such as grease) that is capable of reducing friction, heat, and wear when introduced as a film between solid surfaces. As such, lubricants are crucial for DIYers wanting to keep things running smoothly around their home and in their car or truck.

When you go to the hardware store of home center to buy a lubricant, you'll be amazed at the number of options. And there's a reason why there are so many!

Each lubricant is formulated for a specific job and that particular lubricant usually provides far better results and wear protection than a general-purpose product or a product designed for a different job. And, a specialty product usually lasts much longer. So, by using the right lube, you'll lubricate less often, avoid frustrations and save time and money.

....

➤ Silicone lubricant dries quickly and invisibly, and it doesn't attract dirt so it's perfect for drawer rollers, window tracks, door locks and bike parts.

➤ Lithium grease is a bit messy, but it's also long-lasting and weather-resistant which makes it good to use on garage door tracks, car doors and latches and other metal parts that get heavy use outdoors.

➤ WD40 is the multipurpose lubricant that is a must-have for DIYers. Do you know what WD40 stands for? In 1953, the Rocket Chemical Company made 40 attempts to create a water displacing formula for the aerospace industry. It was the 40th attempt that worked and the rest is history!

Lubrication shop chart

LUBE TYPE	BEST USES	ADVANTAGES	DISADVANTAGES
All-purpose lube	Frees up lightly rusted tools and dissolves light rust. Lubricates light-duty mechanisms like drawer slides and hinges. Dissolves some adhesives and removes scuff marks from floors. Removes pressure-sensitive adhesive labels.	Safe for wood, metal and plastic. Works fast. Dissolves gummed-up old lube and relubricates. Flows quickly and penetrates deep into tight spaces. Protects against corrosion.	Lubrication and rust protection don't last long—you may have to reapply frequently. Not for use on rubber products. Not for heavy loads or high-torque applications. Attracts and retains dust and dirt. Works very slowly to free up nuts and bolts.
Dry PTFE lube	Light-load lubrication for drawer slides, rollers, hinges, hand tools, window tracks/mechanisms, latches and lock cylinders	Won't gather dust or dirt. Once solvent evaporates, product stays in place (won't drip). Safe for wood, metal, most types of plastic and rubber.	No corrosion protection. Not for heavy loads or high-torque applications.
Spray silicone	Light-load lubrication for things that slide or roll—drawer slides, hinges, hand tools, window tracks/mechanisms, electrical connectors, weather stripping, etc. Prevents sticking on mower decks and snow blower chutes.	Slipperiest of all lubes. Repels liquid water (not water vapor). Stays wet and continues to spread with every sliding movement.	Remains tacky and holds dust and dirt. No corrosion protection. Once applied, the surface is unpaintable. Overspray makes floors dangerously slippery.
Lithium grease	Medium- to high-load applications like axles, rollers, bearings, spinning shafts on shop and garden equipment, and hinges that carry a heavy load. Any lubrication job where the lube must stay in place.	Lasts far longer than oil. Stays in place and doesn't drip. Aerosol versions allow grease to seep into tight places so you don't have to disassemble items to apply grease. Protects against corrosion.	Remains tacky and holds dust and dirt. Washes off in heavy rain.
Marine grease	Trailer wheel bearings, shafts, rollers and gears immersed in water and continually exposed to the elements. Prevents rust and seizing of metal parts.	Handles high loads and torque. Stays in place. Most water resistant of any grease.	Remains tacky and holds dust and dirt.
Synthetic grease	High-load, high-torque lubricant for axles, bearings, gears or spinning shafts in power tools and equipment.	Lowest friction of all greases. Most resistant to breakdown under high heat. Stays in place. Dissipates heat well.	Remains tacky and holds dust and dirt. Most expensive of all consumer-type greases.
Chain lube	Bicycle, motorcycle and scooter drive chains. Garage door opener chain and outdoor power equipment chains.	Penetrates deep into roller links when first applied. Becomes tack-free and sling-free once dry, so it holds far less dust and dirt than other lubes.	Doesn't spread once dry. May harm plastic or rubber (check the label before spraying chains that contain nonmetal parts).
Garage door lube	Garage door hinges, rollers, cables, reels and springs.	Penetrates, lubricates and protects against corrosion. Less tacky, so less likely to hold dirt.	May harm plastic or rubber parts.
Penetrating oil	Frees up rusty tools, tracks, slides, nuts and bolts.	Fastest option to break up rust and free fasteners. Dissolves grease and old, gummy lubricant.	Not a good permanent lubricant. Some formulas may dissolve paint or damage finishes.

Lubrication tips

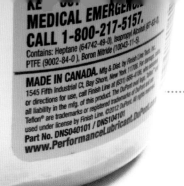

Shake before using. All spray and squeeze bottle lubes contain solvents along with the actual lubricant. If you don't shake the product before application, you'll get a lot of solvent and very little lube.

Avoid the off-brands. Cheap brands cost less for a reason— they contain less of what matters. These two beakers show how much silicone was left after the solvents and propellants evaporated from a name-brand product and a cheaper "no-name" brand.

pro tips!

➤ **Clean out the old lube.** Adding fresh lube to old, degraded oil and grease is a prescription for equipment failure. To get the full advantage of fresh lube, always clean out the old lube with spray solvent and a rag (aerosol brake cleaner works well).

Prevent seizing. Apply a thin coat of marine grease to a trailer hitch ball mount to prevent it from rusting and "welding" itself to the receiver.

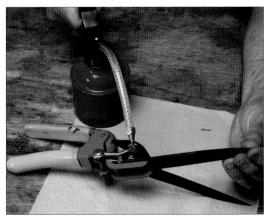

Lithium grease for garden equipment. Lubricate heavy garden equipment wheels with spray lithium grease. It'll stand up to the load better than oil, silicone or PTFE. Take the wheel off and spread grease on by hand or shoot it with aerosol white lithium grease. Spin the wheel to work the lube into the axle before the solvent evaporates.

Don't forget plain old motor oil. That leftover can of 30-weight motor oil isn't the very best lube for all jobs, but it's a handy and acceptable friction fighter for most. Heavyweight motor oil is thicker than most spray oils, so it provides a stronger film cushion. And motor oil has built-in anticorrosive additives to resist rust. Since it doesn't have any solvents, a full drop is really a full drop of lube. And it's cheap—a quart should last a lifetime.

Choose dry lube for dusty situations. Dusty and dirty conditions call for a lube that isn't tacky. Dry PTFE is a good choice for this vacuum cleaner. It dries tack-free and bonds well to surfaces, so the spinning parts won't throw off lubricant.

Grease, not oil, for high loads. Reduce wear on gears and bearings with a heavy-duty synthetic grease. Spread it on all surfaces and rotate the parts by hand to distribute the grease. Never pack the gear case completely full unless directed by the manufacturer.

Clean and Restore

YOUR COST: $12
(plus $40/day rental
if you don't own a
pressure washer)

SAVINGS:
$288 ($248)

COMPLEXITY
Moderate

TOOLS
Pressure washer

6- to 12-ft.
  extension rod

Ladder

Brush with 4-ft.
  handle

Bucket

Garden hose

MATERIALS
Bleach (for mold)

Detergent

TSP

Pressure wash
your whole house

Whether you're prepping your house for painting or you've noticed that your
home's exterior is dingy and needs freshening, a pressure washer will make the
job go faster and easier.

A pressure washer is a tremendous time-saving tool. Its high-velocity water
spray cleans dirt, grime and chalking paint from otherwise sound painted surfaces.
Pro painters like pressure washers not only because they're fast, but because they
scour the old paint so the new coat will adhere better.

START ABOUT 2' FROM SIDING

Practice handling the washer in a low area first. Hold the wand with two hands and move it across the siding from side to side at a steady pace. Start about 2 ft. from the siding, then move closer until you find the optimal cleaning distance. In general, work at a horizontal or slightly down-ward angle to avoid driving water up under the siding.

Pressure washing works on wood, vinyl, aluminum siding and masonry, but due to its high pressure, we don't recommend it for hardboard siding. Hard-board is more vulnerable to moisture than wood is and extremely difficult to repair if you accidentally damage it.

Pressure washing won't stop mildew. (It'll wash most of it away, but the mildew will soon grow back.) To get rid of mildew so it doesn't come back, use a scrub brush instead of the pressure washer and wash the area with a mixture of 1 part bleach to 9 parts water.

CAUTION: KEEP WELL AWAY FROM ELECTRICAL DEVICES

REMOVE NUMBERS

Begin washing walls at the top and work down. Wash the gutters and soffits as well as the siding. Direct the spray away from breakable objects like windows and outside lights, and remove house numbers and window boxes before you start, if possible.

Rent or buy a washer that produces at least 2,000 psi (pounds per square inch) of pressure. You don't have to be experienced to use a pressure washer, but be prepared for a day of physical labor. The washer will probably be gas powered and weigh more than 75 lbs. If you rent a pressure washer, ask the rental agent to show you how to hook it up and operate it, and to review safety precautions with you.

Pressure washers look like the ultimate squirt gun, but they aren't toys. Don't point them at anyone or try to rinse your hands or feet. They can tear your skin. If you don't feel confident operating it, hire a pro, who will wash an average-size house for about $300.

Finally, make sure you get a 6- to 12-ft. extension wand to help reach high areas.

ANGLE SPRAY AWAY FROM WINDOWS

CAUTION

Pressure washing is not a safe paint prep method if the exterior paint contains lead. If your home was built before 1978 (when lead paint for residential housing was banned) or if you're unsure, have your paint tested or contact your local health department for safe handling instructions.

Direct the nozzle away from windows, holding the wand at an angle so you don't drive water into joints, gaps or against the glass. Even so, check the sill on the inside and dry up any water that leaked through. Remove the shutters after washing and wash underneath.

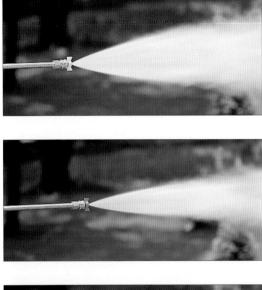

25-DEGREE NOZZLE

15-DEGREE NOZZLE

0-DEGREE NOZZLE (DON'T USE)

Selecting the best nozzle

Pressure washers usually have three or four nozzles with spray patterns of varying widths. Attach the 15- or 25-degree nozzle to the wand for general paint removal and cleaning, then test the effect on the siding. The spray should clean away all dirt and chalk without damaging the siding. Don't use the narrow, zero-degree nozzle. It's powerful and can quickly damage wood, stucco and other materials

CAUTION

Make sure the nozzle coupling locks into place securely so you don't blow the nozzle through a neighbor's window!

pro tips!

➤ While it's best to wash with the wand aimed downward, at times you'll have to point it somewhat upward, especially under soffits. When you do, remember the general rule not to drive the water directly into cracks or gaps. And always avoid shooting water up into soffit vents.

➤ We don't recommend that you pressure wash while standing on a ladder; the recoil from the pressure can knock you off balance.

➤ Steer clear of electrical devices like lights and outlets. You can easily cause a short circuit or break them.

➤ If you're planning to paint, give your house at least a week of good drying weather before applying paint.

BRUSH WITH 4' HANDLE

LADDER STABILIZER

GARDEN HOSE

KEEP SIDING DAMP BELOW

Clean high areas beyond the reach of the pressure washer extension with a scrub brush and a solution of detergent and TSP mixed in water. Begin from the lower areas and work upward, rinsing frequently. Keep the siding below damp so the TSP won't leave visible drip marks. When finished, rinse from the top down using a garden hose. An add-on ladder stabilizer makes the ladder more secure.

Water-stained brick

Those hard-water stains left behind by your sprinkler can be tenacious. Generally, they're composed of calcium carbonate and you'll need an acid-based cleaner to get rid of them. However, don't use muriatic acid (which is commonly suggested), because it can stain or bleach many colors of brick and cause aluminum window frames to corrode.

Instead, several brick cleaners are available that, because of special buffers, work well without the staining problem. Look for products made by ProSoCo and Diedrich.

When you clean the brick, remember that you are using an acid-based product and follow all precautions and directions. After cleaning your brick, avoid some future headaches by sealing it with a siloxane or silane-based sealer. For more information on cleaning brick, visit the Brick Institute of America at gobrick.com.

PROFESSIONAL COST: $300

YOUR COST: $15

 SAVINGS: $285

COMPLEXITY
Simple

TOOLS
Stiff brush with handle

Bucket

Garden hose

MATERIALS
Brick cleaner

Plastic tarp

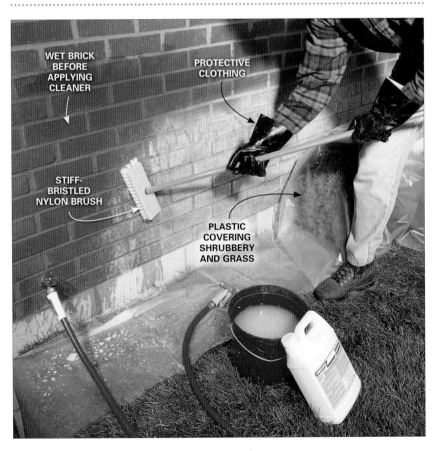

WET BRICK BEFORE APPLYING CLEANER

PROTECTIVE CLOTHING

STIFF-BRISTLED NYLON BRUSH

PLASTIC COVERING SHRUBBERY AND GRASS

Restoring dingy stucco

Stucco, a durable cement-based material that is used on exteriors as well as interior walls and ceilings, is made up of Portland cement, sand and water. If your home has a stucco exterior, don't use ordinary house paint on it. Paint can form a nonbreathable film on stucco, which will cause the paint to pop off when moisture migrates through the wall.

When a stucco exterior needs refreshing, the process is called "redashing." This involves adding new layers of stucco over the existing surface, and is usually only done by pros.

However, if you have a small area of stucco that is stained and needs a touch up, you can use a whitewash to freshen it up. To make whitewash, mix white Portland cement (available at most lumberyards) and water in a pail to the consistency of pancake batter. Wet the stucco with a garden hose and apply the whitewash with a masonry brush or whisk broom. You can color the whitewash by adding masonry dye, which is available from brick suppliers. An exact color match is almost impossible, so plan to whitewash an entire wall for the best results.

MASONRY
BRUSH

JOINT
COMPOUND
MIXER

WHITE PORTLAND
CEMENT

MIXING
BUCKET

Bathroom exhaust fan

If the grille on your bathroom exhaust fan is clogged with dust, there is a more effective way to clean it than by vacuuming: Turn on the fan and blast out the dust with "canned air." The fan will blow the dust outside. This works on the return air grilles of your central heating/cooling system too. Run the system so that the return airflow will carry the dust to the filter. You'll find canned air at home centers and hardware stores, usually in the electrical supplies aisle.

PROFESSIONAL COST: $50

YOUR COST: $5

SAVINGS: $45

COMPLEXITY
Simple

TOOLS
Ladder

MATERIALS
Canned air

CAUTION

The cans contain chemical propellants, not just air. Don't let children play with them.

COMPLEXITY
Simple

TOOLS
Car wash mitt

Soft-bristle brush

Bucket

Towels

MATERIALS
WD-40

Car washing soap

Spray-on solution

Clay bar lubricant

Car exterior detailing

Attention to detail when you're cleaning your vehicle's exterior can keep it looking new and prevent premature rust and a dull finish. In most cases, you can do a complete cleaning and detailing job in less than three hours. You'll not only enjoy driving a good-looking car but you'll also find that a well-detailed car can bring as much as $400 to $500 over book value when you decide to sell. Along with describing washing and waxing basics, we'll show you techniques that pros use to revive cars for resale.

1. **Tired of your bumper stickers?** Soak the sticker in warm soapy water for at least 10 minutes, then take a plastic putty knife and get under a corner and start working it loose. Never use a metal scraper or razor blade because they can scratch the finish. If the sticker still won't budge, wipe off the soap solution and give the sticker a spray of WD-40, let it absorb and start scraping again. The WD-40 will loosen the adhesive and act as a lubricant for the putty knife without harming your car's finish. Keep spraying as needed if you run into stubborn spots. Once the sticker is removed, you may have adhesive still stuck to the bumper. Dab rubbing alcohol onto a clean rag and scrub

until the residue is gone. Wash and dry the area, then put on a coat of wax.

2. **Wash the entire car one section at a time.** Soak the entire car with your hose to get rid of loose dirt and dust,

a soft-bristled washing brush to get at areas where a rag or mitt can get caught (racks and license plate brackets, door handles, trim, etc.). Open the hood and trunk and wash the crevices where dirt gets trapped. When you've finished washing the last section, rinse the whole car again and then dry it with a chamois, starting from the top down. Wring out the chamois often to keep it absorbent. The idea is to avoid water spots and streaks.

3. **Use a spray-on solution to clean door-jambs and weather stripping.** You can use a hose and bucket, but it's often tough to keep water from spraying into the interior. A spray-on wash is great for this because you'll have a lot more control and won't be flooding delicate door mechanisms with water. Get into all the nooks and crannies around the weather strip and hinges to make your car look showroom perfect.

4. **Scrub the wheels and tires with a brush.** Ordinary soap and water often aren't enough to get rid of caked-on brake dust and road grime, so buy a specialty cleaner for your type of wheels (painted, chrome, alloy or clear coat). Spray the wheel and let the solution work for about 30 seconds, then scrub with a soft-bristled brush to work the cleaner into all the small recesses. Flush with water and repeat the process if necessary. After you've cleaned the tires to make them look show-room new, put a coat of wax on the wheels. Spray-on wax works best.

5. **Revive a dull paint finish.** Contamination from brake dust and air pollution dulls painted finishes and eventually leads to surface rust. The best way to revive the finish is with a clay bar that actually absorbs these contaminants as you rub it back and

and use a heavy jet spray under the wheel wells where road dirt accumulates. Then fill a bucket with warm water and add car-washing soap. Dish soap is generally too harsh. Avoiding the direct sun, wash a section at a time and then rinse it immediately. Start from the top down: first the roof, then the hood, the trunk and finally the sides. Use a special wash mitt or a heavy terry cloth towel. Work the soapy water in a circular motion and get into corners and detail lines. Use

forth across the paint. Professional detailers have been using this product for years. Now you can find it at auto supply stores or online. Spray the surface with either the lubricant that comes with your clay bar or liquid wax. Never use plain water. Rub the clay back and forth on the freshly lubricated section, overlapping each stroke and using light pressure. It will sound harsh at first,but as the clay bar absorbs contaminants, it will get quieter and smoother. Rework as needed until the finish feels as smooth as glass. Remove any residue by spraying on more lubricant and then buff with a clean terry cloth towel.

6. **Wax your car at least twice a year.** Very lightly mist a 2- x 2-ft. section with clean water and then apply a good-quality wax. Do a panel at a time, such as the hood or the roof, just as you do when you wash. Apply the wax with the applicator, rubbing in a circular motion. Let the wax dry to a haze and remove it with a lint-free, soft terry towel. Open the the doors, the hood and the trunk to remove haze from the edges. Never wax in direct sun.

7. **Give your weather stripping renewed life.** Clean door, trunk and hood weathe stripping with a protective silicone spray. Wash the weather strip first, then apply the protectant to a rag (prepackaged wipes are available) and work it into the weather strip until it shines. You'll restore its suppleness, protect it from aging and keep it from freezing to the door in icy winter weather.

CLAY BAR LUBRICANT

CLAY BAR

pro tips!

➤ **Forget the sponge, use a microfiber mitt.** Sponges capture and hold dirt and grit in their large pores. You can wring it out, but the grit will stay put. Once grit is embedded, you may as well wash your car with sandpaper. A car detailer will use a microfiber car wash mitt because the grit falls out when you rinse. Once you've mixed the suds, go one step further—fill a second bucket with clean rinse water. Use it to rinse the wash mitt often. That'll remove most of the road grit from the mitt to prevent scratches. When you're finished, throw the mitt in the washing machine to get it completely clean.

➤ **Rinse before you reload.** Swish the wash mitt in clean water before you reload it with fresh suds. Dump and refill the rinse bucket with clean water before you start washing the opposite side of the vehicle.

PROFESSIONAL
COST: $125

YOUR COST: $35

SAVINGS: $90

COMPLEXITY
Simple

TOOLS
Vacuum

Carpet cleaning
  machine

Artist's brush

Plastic putty knife

MATERIALS
Carpet cleaning soap
  or spray

Leather conditioner

Goo-Gone

Deodorizer

Car interior detailing

Unless you're fastidious about your car's interior, it's usually one of the last things on your to-do list. So whether it's time to sell your car or you're tired of the mess, these tips from professional detailers will give you the most return for your energy.

1. **Slide the seat all the way forward and clean out all the junk underneath.** Vacuum the seats, remove the mats and vacuum the carpet. Use a brush attachment for the dash and door panels. Don't forget to clean out and vacuum those handy door pockets.

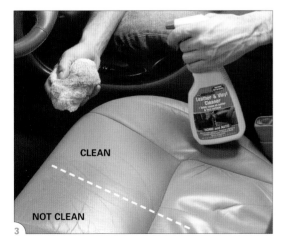

CARPET DEEP-CLEANING MACHINE

2

HAND METHOD

CLEAN

NOT CLEAN

3

2. **Deep-clean carpeting and upholstery.**
Use a carpet cleaning machine to get the deep dirt that settles into the fibers of the carpet. (Clean cloth seats this way as well.) It sprays the carpet with a solution of water and cleaner and then sucks the dirt and grime into a reservoir. A machine like this pays for itself after just a few uses. You can also rent one from a rental center or use a spray-on cleaner and a scrub brush instead.

3. **Clean and condition the leather or vinyl.** After a couple of years, you'll notice that the color of the leather seats no longer matches the rest of the interior. It's not enough just to condition the leather. First spray on leather cleaner and rub vigorously with a clean terry cloth towel. To avoid rubbing the grime back into the seats, keep flipping the cloth to expose a fresh surface. Let the seats dry for an hour and then rub in a leather conditioner to keep the leather supple.

4. **Remember to get into the nooks and crannies.** Detailing means just that—finding and dealing with all the trim lines and recesses that a quick once-over cleaning job misses. Wrap a cloth around an old, worn screwdriver (without sharp edges) and spray an all-purpose cleaner on the cloth. Move it gently along the trim lines to pick up the gunk. Keep refreshing the surface of the cloth. Go around all the buttons and controls as well. Follow up with a rejuvenator.

5. **Brush out the air vents.** These louvers are a real magnet for dust, and a vacuum with a brush attachment just won't get it all. Take an inexpensive paint brush and give it a light shot of furniture polish. Work the brush into the crevices to collect the dust. Wipe the brush off with a rag and move on to the next vent.

6. **Wash the windows, including the top edges.** Ever notice that line of grime on the tops of windows when they're partially rolled down? Most people overlook this detail when giving their vehicle a quick wash. A few minutes with glass cleaner and a clean rag is all it takes.

4

LONG-BRISTLED
ARTIST'S BRUSH

5

GRIME AT TOP
OF WINDOW

6

PLASTIC PUTTY KNIFE

7

7. **Scrape off those annoying stickers.** While all of your national and state park stickers may call to mind great memories, they can be a visual hazard as they accumulate. The high-quality stickers will pull off if you can get under a corner and carefully pull them free at a 90-degree angle. Others will leave a gummy residue and require a bit more attention. Cover your dash with an old towel and dab on a goo remover. Then scrape and wipe it off.

8. **Kill bad odors.** Whether your vehicle smells like fast-food hamburgers or cigarettes, a couple pumps of a car deodorizer will solve the problem.

ODOR ELIMINATOR

8

Central air conditioner

A year's worth of dirt and debris clogging the cooling fins, a low coolant level, a dirty blower fan filter and a number of other simple problems can significantly reduce the efficiency of your air conditioner and wear it out faster. Only a pro can check the coolant level, but you can easily handle most of the routine cleaning chores. Here you'll learn how to clean the outdoor unit (called the condenser) and the accessible parts of the indoor unit (called the evaporator). All the steps are simple and straightforward and will take you only a few hours total. You don't need any special skills, tools or experience. You may have a different type of central air conditioner than we show here—a heat pump system, for example, or a unit mounted horizontally in the attic. However, you can still carry out most maintenance procedures we show here, because each system will have a condenser outside and an evaporator inside.

Clean the outdoor unit

BLOCK SHUTOFF

1. Always begin by shutting off the electrical power to the unit. Normally you'll find a shutoff nearby. It may be a switch in a box, a pull lever or a fuse block that you pull out. Look for the "on-off" markings. If you're in doubt, shut off the power at the main electrical panel.

2. Vacuum the fins clean with a soft brush. They're fragile and easily bent or crushed. On many units you'll have to unscrew and lift off a metal box to get at them. Check your owner's manual for directions and lift off the box carefully to avoid bumping the fins. Also, clear away all bushes, weeds and grass within 2 ft. of the condenser.

3. Occasionally you'll find fins that have been bent. Minor straightening can be done with a dinner knife. Don't insert the knife more than 1/2 in. If large areas of fins are crushed, have a pro straighten them during a routine service call.

pro tips!

> Call for service before the first heat wave, when the pros become swamped with repair calls!

4. Now, unscrew the top grille and lift out the fan to gain access to the interior of the condenser. You can't completely remove it because its wiring is connected to the unit. You might need a helper to hold it while you vacuum debris from the inside. (Sometimes mice like to over-winter there!) Pull out any leaves and wipe the interior surfaces clean with a damp cloth.

5. Now hose off the fins. Spray the fins using moderate water pressure from a hose nozzle. Direct the spray from the inside out. Reinstall the fan.

6. Turn the power back on, then set the house thermostat to "cool" so the compressor comes on. After 10 minutes, feel the insulated tube. It should feel cool. The uninsulated tube should feel warm. Now you can move inside to finish the cleaning process.

FAN

ELECTRICAL WIRES

4

5

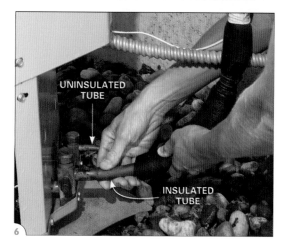

UNINSULATED TUBE

INSULATED TUBE

6

7

SHUTOFF SWITCH

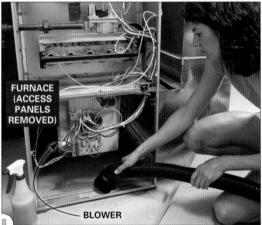

8

FURNACE (ACCESS PANELS REMOVED)

BLOWER

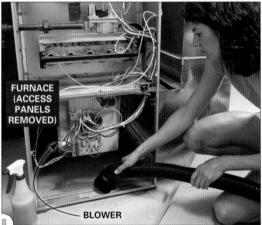

9

DRAIN PORT

FLEXIBLE DRAIN TUBE

DRAIN PORT

DRAIN TUBE

Clean the indoor unit

7. Begin by turning off the power to the furnace or blower. Usually you'll find a simple toggle switch nearby in a metal box, otherwise turn the power off at the main electrical panel. If you have trouble opening the blower unit or finding the filter, check your owner's manual for help. The manual will also list the filter type, but if it's your first time changing the filter, take the old one with you when buying a new one to make sure you get the right size. Be sure to keep the power to the blower off whenever you remove the filter. Otherwise you'll blow dust into the evaporator fins.

8. The evaporator usually sits in an inaccessible spot inside a metal duct downstream from the blower. If you can get to it, gently vacuum its fins (from the blower side) with a soft brush as you did with the condenser.

9. The evaporator fins dehumidify the air as they cool it, so you'll find a tube to drain the condensation. The water collects in a pan and drains out the side. Most tubes are flexible plastic and are easy to pull off and clean. Clean it by pouring a bleach/water solution (1:16 ratio) through the tube to flush the line. Poke a pipe cleaner into the drain port and clean out any debris. Reinstall the drain tube and turn the power back on.

PROFESSIONAL
COST: $500

YOUR COST: $150

SAVINGS: $350

COMPLEXITY
Simple

TOOLS
Sponge mop

Broom handle

Polyester brush

Paint tray

Paint pad

MATERIALS
Floor restoration kit

Painter's tape

Restore wood floors

If the finish on your wood floor is worn and lightly scratched, you can make it look like new without the labor, mess and expense of sanding off the finish. You can use this floor renewal method on wood floors that you would otherwise have to sand or on flooring that's difficult or impossible to sand, such as prefinished or laminated wood. You can also use it on plastic laminate flooring. Professional floor refinishers have used this "chemical etching" process for years, and now there's a system designed for a novice.

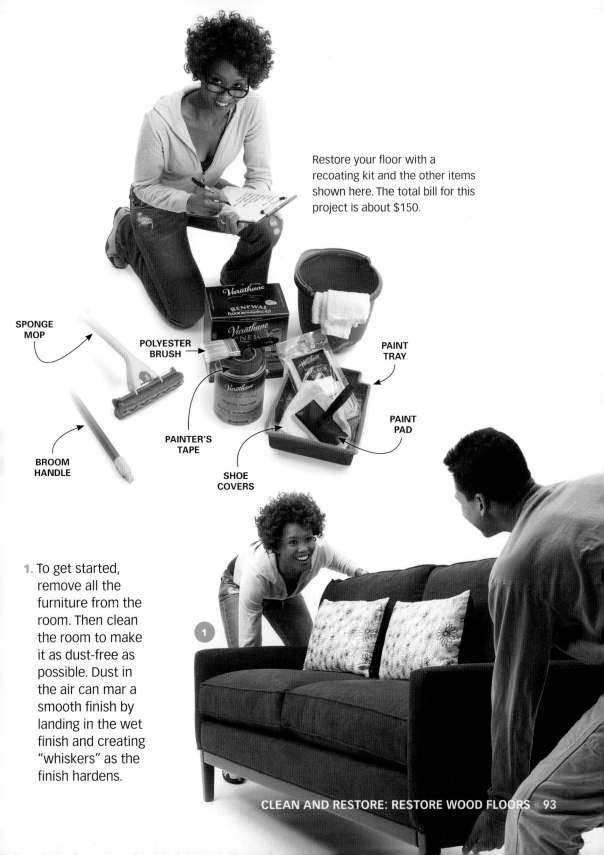

Restore your floor with a recoating kit and the other items shown here. The total bill for this project is about $150.

SPONGE MOP

POLYESTER BRUSH

PAINT TRAY

PAINT PAD

BROOM HANDLE

PAINTER'S TAPE

SHOE COVERS

1. To get started, remove all the furniture from the room. Then clean the room to make it as dust-free as possible. Dust in the air can mar a smooth finish by landing in the wet finish and creating "whiskers" as the finish hardens.

2. To limit air movement, close windows, turn off the ceiling fan or window air conditioner, and block any ducts in the room.

3. Scrub a small section of floor with the abrasive pad and the liquid etcher. Scrub with the grain, applying firm pressure.

BROOM HANDLE

APPLICATOR BLOCK

ABRASIVE PAD

4. Wipe up the excess liquid etcher as soon as you're done scrubbing each section. Then move on to the next section.

Is this system right for your floor?

This process will make some floors look absolutely perfect. Others will look much better, though not quite perfect. Still others are not good candidates for this process at all and require sanding instead. The category your floor falls into depends on the amount and type of damage it has.

➤ Normal wear and shallow scratches in the finish only (not the wood) are no problem; they'll disappear under the new coat of finish.

➤ Deeper scratches that go through the finish and into the wood won't disappear completely, even if you touch them up with stain (Photo 8). A shiny new coat of finish may even accentuate deep scratches and dents. There's no harm in applying new finish over these spots. But if your floor has a lot of deep damage, sanding is your best option.

➤ If you have heavy traffic paths where the finish is completely worn away or areas where the finish is flaking off (often caused by water damage), don't use this process. The etching chemical can discolor bare wood and won't remove water stains.

➤ If your floor has been waxed or has a wax finish, the new finish won't stick. To check for wax, find a low-traffic spot behind a door or near an inside corner. Place a few drops of mineral spirits on the floor; let it stand for two to three minutes, and then wipe it off with a clean white rag. If the rag shows any brown or shiny residue, you've got wax. In that case, sanding is your best option. Alternatively, you can buff on a fresh coat of wax for a fresh, although temporary, shine.

5. Walk the dog for 30 minutes while you're waiting for the etching liquid to dry.

6. Damp-mop the floor with water and dish-washing liquid to neutralize the liquid etcher. Wear shoe covers to keep the floor clean.

SHOE COVER

7. Take a 30-minute coffee break, allowing the damp floor to dry completely.

8. Touch up any scratches that have cut through the finish into the wood. Apply stain and dry it with a hair dryer. Then brush on a light coat of finish and dry it.

OIL-BASED STAIN

FLOOR FINISH

9. Plan your strategy so you don't paint yourself into a corner. Have your helper work along walls with a paint pad while you follow close behind with the applicator pad.

pro tips!

➤ To make the applicator pad, brushes and paint pads more pliable and responsive right from the start, rinse them in water, then dry them until they are just damp to the touch.

DRY SIDE →

EXCESS
FINISH

10

LIGHT
TOUCH ←

11

10. Gently plow the finish with the grain of the wood. Pull the applicator at an angle so the excess finish puddles on the dry side of the floor.

11. Smooth out drips or puddles with a polyester brush. Stick close to the "pad person" to fix drips before they begin to dry.

12. Watch a long movie, allowing the finish to dry for at least three hours before you apply an optional second coat.

Your final finish will be hard enough for "sock traffic" after eight hours, and ready for you to move furniture back after 24 hours. Give your floor two weeks to completely cure before putting down an area rug.

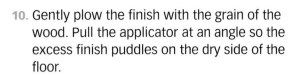

12

Chapter 4

How to Paint

How to paint a ceiling

Ceilings present some unique painting challenges. For starters, they're large and often illuminated with light that accentuates even the smallest flaw in the paint. Add to that the challenge of working overhead and things can get messy in a hurry. These tips will help you do a great job even if this is the first time you've painted a ceiling.

PROFESSIONAL COST: $300

YOUR COST: $45

SAVINGS: $255

COMPLEXITY
Simple

TOOLS
Extension pole

1/2-in. lambswool
   roller cover

Roller frame

Trim brush

Paint tray

MATERIALS
Primer

Paint

1. **Buy special ceiling paint.** While there are exceptions, in general you'll get the best results with paint that's formulated for a ceiling application. For a ceiling, you want paint that doesn't spatter, has a long open time (which means it dries slowly), and is flat instead of glossy. Most ceiling paints are formulated with these qualities. And of course you can have ceiling paint tinted if you want a color other than "ceiling white."

2. **Don't be afraid of color.** You may not want to paint your ceiling yellow, but don't be afraid to deviate from plain old white. Painting the ceiling a color can make a small room seem bigger, or a room with a high ceiling seem more intimate. Plus, it's just more interesting. Ask at any full-service paint store for help in choosing complementary wall and ceiling colors, or search online for examples of rooms you like.

3. **Use a stain-blocking primer to cover flaws.** Roof leaks, overflowing sinks, tobacco smoke and big spills can all leave ugly ceiling stains or dinginess that is impossible to conceal with regular paint. But cover the stain with a coat of stain-blocking primer and your troubles are over. We recommend white pigmented shellac. You can buy spray cans of pigmented shellac, but we prefer brushing it on. Just don't forget to pick up some ammonia or denatured alcohol to clean your brush. If you're painting over a ceiling that's yellow from smoke, roll a coat of shellac over the entire ceiling before painting with latex paint.

4. **Sand before you paint**. Over time, and as the layers of paint build up, bumps and crud can get stuck to the ceiling. On untextured ceilings, start with a quick once-over sanding with 100-grit drywall sanding paper. This helps ensure a perfectly smooth paint job and increases paint bonding. The easiest way to do this is with a sanding pole. When you're done sanding, wipe the ceiling with a damp sponge to remove the dust.

5. **Cut in before you roll.** Cutting in refers to the practice of using a paint brush to paint the edges of a wall or ceiling before you roll the rest of the surface. We recommend carefully brushing paint along the edge of the ceiling a section at a time. Cut in about 10 linear feet and then roll that section. This method has an advantages over cutting in the entire room at once: the cut-in section will remain wet until you roll, so it blends in better.

6. **Lap your cut-in onto the walls.** If you're planning to paint the walls too, lap the paint onto the walls a little bit when you're cutting in. Then when you paint the walls, you can err on the side of leaving a little ceiling color showing when you cut in and it won't be noticeable.

7. **You don't need an expensive pole.** You can buy all kinds of fancy extendable paint poles, but a simple wooden broom handle works just as well.

pro tips!

➤ **Clear the room.** Move everything out of the room and cover the floors with drop cloths before painting a ceiling. If this isn't possible, group furniture in the center and cover it with painter's plastic. Sometimes it may be necessary to make two or more small groups so that you can reach over them with the roller.

8. **Use a thick, premium roller cover.** This tip applies to most paint jobs but is even more important for ceilings. You want to get as much paint on the ceiling as you can in the shortest amount of time possible while minimizing spatters. To do this, you need the best roller cover you can buy. We recommend a 1/2-in.-nap lambswool cover. These covers do cost more but they are easy to clean and can last a long time if you take good care of them.

9. **Roll both directions.** There are a few tricks to getting a smooth, consistent coat of paint on the ceiling. First, work in sections about 5 or 6 ft. square. Move quickly from one section to the next to make sure the paint along the edge doesn't dry before you roll the adjoining section. This is called "keeping a wet edge" and is the key to avoiding lap marks. You'll get the best coverage by immediately rerolling each section at a right angle to your first roller direction as you go.

10

10. Roll gently on textured ceilings. Painting textured ceilings is a bit of a crapshoot. If the texture has been painted over already, it's probably safe to paint again. If the texture has never been painted, there's a risk the water in the paint could loosen the texture, causing it to fall off in sheets. A lot depends on the quality of the texturing job. If you have a closet or other inconspicuous area, do a test by rolling on some paint to see what happens. If the texture loosens, painting over the larger ceiling is risky. When painting a textured ceiling, avoid overworking the paint. Just roll the paint on and leave it. Don't go back and forth with the roller, as this is likely to pull the texture from the ceiling. If the ceiling needs another coat of paint, wait for the first coat to dry completely. Then roll another coat perpendicular to the first one using the same careful technique. If you want to remove the ceiling texture, see p. 188.

Paint a panel door

The actual work involved in painting a paneled door typically amounts to three to five hours, depending on the condition of the door and how fussy you are. But add in the drying time and it's a full-day project. So if you're painting a door you can't live without—like a bathroom or exterior door—get started first thing in the morning so it can be back in service by day's end.

While you're picking a paint color, also think about sheen: With a flat finish, scuff marks and handprints are hard to wipe away. High gloss is easy to clean but accentuates every little flaw, so your prep and paint job have to be perfect. Satin and semigloss are good compromise choices. Also check the operation of the door. If it rubs against the jamb or drags on the carpet, now's the time to sand or plane the edges. If you have several doors that need painting, start with the least prominent one. It's better to make learning mistakes on the inside of a closet door than on your entry door.

Prep tips

➤ You'll get better results if you remove the door rather than painting it in place.

➤ Working in your garage, shop or basement, you can control lighting and drying conditions better.

➤ Laying the door flat minimizes runs in the paint job.

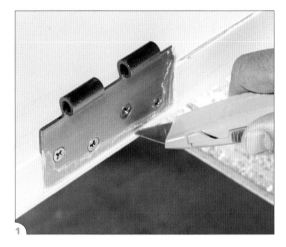

**HARD RUBBER
SANDING
BLOCK**

1. Clean the door with a household cleaner. Almost any cleaner will do, as long as it cuts grease. Areas around doorknobs are especially prone to greasy buildup. Slice through paint buildup around hinges and latches and remove all of the door hardware to get a neater paint job and save time. To remove old paint from the hardware, start with a product intended to remove paint splatter (GoofOff is one brand). You can use paint strippers, but they may also remove clear coatings from the hardware or damage the finish. If you're dealing with more than one door, avoid hardware mix-ups by labeling plastic bags that will hold the hardware for each door.

Fill dents and holes with a sandable filler.

2. If your door is in good shape, all it needs is a light sanding with sandpaper (180 or 220 grit) or a sanding sponge. That will roughen the surface a little and allow the primer to adhere better. But most likely, you'll also need to smooth out chipped paint and imperfections from previous paint jobs. This is usually the most time-consuming, tedious part of the project. Here are some tips for faster, better results:

➤ Paint often sticks to sandpaper, clogging the grit and making it useless. So be sure to check the label and buy sandpaper intended for paint.

➤ Start with 120- or 150-grit sandpaper. You can switch to coarser paper (80 grit) on problem areas, but be sure to follow up with finer grit to smooth out the sanding scratches.

➤ On flat areas, a hard sanding block will smooth the surface much better than sponges or other soft-backed abrasives.

➤ Buy some sanding sponges and pads for the shaped areas. Through trial and error, you'll find that some work better than others on your profiles.

Tips for a perfect workspace

After the messy job of sanding is done, set the door aside and prep your workspace. For priming and painting, you want a work zone that's well lit and clean. Here's how to prep your space:

➤ Clean everything. Vacuum work surfaces and sweep the floor.

➤ Minimize air movement for less airborne dust and slower drying. Close doors and windows. Turn off forced-air heating or cooling.

➤ Don't rely on overhead lighting; you may even want to turn it off. Instead, position a work light 4 to 5 ft. above the floor. This low-angle light will accentuate any drips or ridges.

➤ Have all your tools and supplies ready, including a pail of water to dunk your paint tools in as soon as you're done.

➤ If you're working in a garage, unplug the garage door opener so it can't be opened while you work. An opening door raises dust.

3. A vacuum with a brush attachment removes most of the dust. Wipe off the rest with a damp rag.

4. Inspect your work with low-angle lighting to accentuate imperfections. If you find any spots that need an extra dab of filler, mark them with tabs of masking tape. When all prep work is done, start with a dust-free door; wipe it down with a damp rag just before painting.

5. Paint all four edges of the door first. Here's why: when painting edges, some paint inevitably slops onto the faces of the door. It's better to have that happen before the faces are painted.

CAUTION

If your home was built before 1979, check the paint for lead before you sand. For more information, go to www.epa.gov/lead.

6. Work the paint into the corners and grooves, then drag the brush over the paint to smooth it.

7. Brush on a light coat. A heavy coat of paint covers better and sometimes levels out better, but runs are more likely and brush marks are deeper. So start out lightly, then lay it on a little thicker as your brush skills improve.

8. Roll on the paint where you can. Rollers lay on paint much faster than a brush, giving you a few more precious minutes to work the paint before it begins to stiffen. Roll the door in sections, coating no more than one-quarter of the door at a time. Then brush out the paint. Be careful not to slop paint over the edges around the panels.

Priming tips

You can "spot-prime" a door, coating only patched dents or areas you sanded through to bare wood. But priming the whole door is best; the new paint will stick better and you'll get a more uniform finish. Here are some tips for this critical step:

➤ Your choice of primer is just as important as your choice of paint. At the paint store, ask for a primer that's compatible with your paint, levels out well and sands smoothly.

➤ Have the primer tinted, based on the color of your paint.

➤ Apply the primer with just as much care as the paint and following the same steps (5–9).

➤ For an ultra-smooth paint job, apply two coats of primer. With a thick layer of primer, you can sand the prime coat glassy-smooth, without sanding through to the old paint.

➤ Lightly sand the primer with 220 grit, inspecting as you go. A couple of quick passes is all it takes. If you're not in a rush to get the door back in service, let the primer dry overnight before sanding. The longer it dries, the better it will sand.

Painting tips

Painting a door is a race against time. You have to lay down the paint and smooth it out before it becomes too sticky to work with, or so stiff that brush marks won't level out and disappear. Keep moving. Don't stop to answer the phone or get coffee. Minutes count. In warm, dry conditions, even seconds matter.

➤ Consider a paint additive to slow down drying and improve leveling. Your paint dealer can recommend one that's compatible with your paint.

➤ Spend a little more and get a quality brush for a smoother finish. We recommend a 2-in. sash brush.

➤ Don't use cheap roller sleeves or you'll get fibers in the finish. Use a mini roller with a microfiber or mohair sleeve. Foam sleeves leave a smooth finish, but they hold very little paint, which slows you down.

Water-based alkyd is best

If you want a smooth finish, choose a paint designed for that. Some paints, even good-quality paints, just aren't formulated for smoothness. Smooth paints are usually labeled "enamel" or "door and trim." But the label alone doesn't tell you enough. Advice from the paint store staff, and the price, are the best indicators. For the smoothest finish, we recommend water-based alkyds. These paints dry slowly for extra working time and level out almost as well as traditional oil-based alkyds. Cleanup is as easy as with any other water-based paint. The disadvantages of water-based alkyds are a very long wait before recoating (16 to 24 hours) and a higher price tag.

9

9. **Brush out rolled paint.** Brushed paint usually levels out better than rolled paint, and any brush marks are less noticeable than roller stipple.

Brush with the grain. Brush across the joints where door parts meet. Then drag your brush in a straight line along the intersection. That way, any visible brush marks will look more like a wood grain pattern and less like sloppy brushwork. Plan to apply at least two coats and lightly sand between coats with 220 grit to remove any dust nubs.

But you might be able to skip the brush-out step altogether. With top-quality enamel and roller sleeves, roller results can be super smooth. This depends in part on drying conditions, so try it on a closet door or a primed scrap of wood first.

pro tips!

LAG SCREW

➤ **Make the door flippable.** Drive one screw into one end and two into the other (above). That lets you coat both sides of the door without waiting for the first side to dry. Drill pilot holes and drive 5/16- x 5-in. lag screws about halfway in.

➤ **Keep a pair of tweezers handy.** Pluck out paintbrush bristles (right) or rescue stuck insects without messing up the paint.

➤ **Wet the floor.** Two benefits for the price of one: A wet floor where you're painting prevents you from kicking up dust that will create dust nubs in your finish. Better yet, it raises the humidity, which extends the time you have to smooth out the paint and it gives the paint more time to level out. (Be careful not to slip on the wet floor!)

PROFESSIONAL
COST: $1,000

YOUR COST: $150

SAVINGS: $110

COMPLEXITY
Moderate

TOOLS
Buckets

Sponges

Sanding sponge

Sanding block

Bright light

Putty knife

Bucket

Brushes

MATERIALS
Non-soapy detergent

Spackling compound

Caulk

Paint

Paint conditioner

Painter's tape

Prep and paint trim like a pro

The old adage, "A good paint job is 90 percent prep work and 10 percent painting," is absolutely true. A quick coat of paint applied over existing paint or stain may look good—but it won't last.

The key to a long-lasting paint job is to prepare the woodwork so it's clean and gloss free. Here we'll show you how to achieve a mar-free surface that'll hold paint for 10 years or even longer. Best of all, the new paint job will look like you had it done by a nitpicky pro.

Whether you're repainting painted wood or painting wood that's been stained and varnished, the steps and tips we show here apply to any woodwork, door, window or trim.

Pro painters know they can't rush a job. Here we'll show you key tips on how the pros remove a surface layer of paint to prepare interior woodwork for optimum adhesion of the new primer and paint.

DIRTY

CLEAN

WASH

RINSE

Step 1: Wash the woodwork

Have two buckets and two scrub sponges (such as Scotch-Brite) at hand, one each for washing solution and clear water rinsing. Don't wash with a cloth rag, as it may shine a flat surface or dull a lustrous one. The goal is to remove the grime so you don't push it farther into the wood during sanding.

Use a non-soapy detergent (such as Dirtex, Spic & Span or TSP No-Rinse Substitute). Dip a scrub sponge into the cleaning solution and wring it out enough to keep it from dripping. Wash wood from the bottom upward with slow, easy up-and-down strokes so the solution has time to soften the grime (top photo). If you start at the top, the cleaner can run down the wood and create hard-to-remove streaks.

Only clean one section at a time so the wood won't dry before you rinse off the cleaner (if directions call for rinsing). To rinse, dip the rinse sponge in clear water and wring it drip free, then wipe the surface clean in one pass. When you begin to wash a new area, start well within the clean area to avoid streaking. Change both the cleaning solution and the rinse water often—whenever the water becomes cloudy.

Spend twice as much time cleaning the wood in areas of high hand contact such as windows, door frames and around light switches and handles/knobs, and places that attract high airborne particles (all wood in kitchens, bathrooms and laundry rooms).

ELBOW GREASE NEEDED HERE

Step 2: Sand and scrape

Hand-sand all woodwork smooth with a fine, 180 grit paper until all shine disappears. A coarser-grit paper will remove more than necessary (use 80 to 120 grit to smooth imperfections such as heavy globs of old paint). If the outside paint layer is gummy, use a "clog-resistant" or "self-lubricating" sandpaper (such as 3M's SandBlaster paper). It has an anti-load coating that keeps the paper from clogging.

Step 3: Buy a sanding block

The right tool improves the sanding job:

- ➤ A folded sheet and finger pressure work great for most areas.
- ➤ A rubber sanding block is comfortable to grip, works well with feathering and lets you apply more even pressure in stubborn areas like windowsills.
- ➤ A sanding sponge or pad conforms readily to curves and crevices. Use fresh sandpaper when you can see paint.

REMOVE
GLOSS

180-GRIT
SPONGE

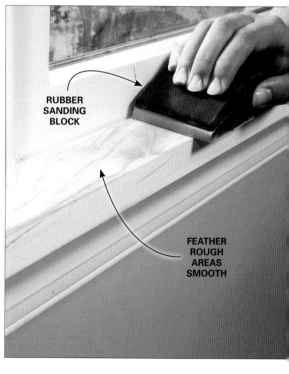

RUBBER
SANDING
BLOCK

FEATHER
ROUGH
AREAS
SMOOTH

Step 4: Fill chips, holes and cracks

Position a hand-held bulb (at least 60 watts) so it shines across (rakes) the wood surface to detect loose paint, rough edges and other blemishes in the surface to determine what needs to be filled. Take a pencil and lightly circle spots that need work.

pro tips!

➤ Perhaps you've moved into a house where the previous owners threw on a quick coat of paint—and now you're stuck redoing it (haven't we all been there!). To determine if the new paint will hold, scribe an "X" lightly into the surface paint layer with a razor blade. Firmly stick duct tape over the mark and yank it away quickly. If any paint adheres to the tape, it's unsound and should be removed.

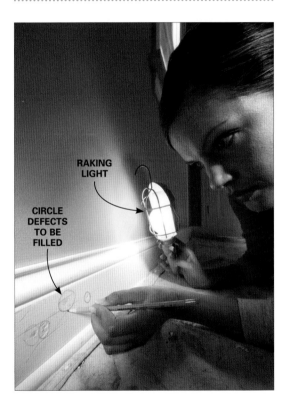

RAKING LIGHT

CIRCLE DEFECTS TO BE FILLED

NO PAINT HERE— LESS SANDING NEEDED

1. **Careful sanding is the key to a perfect job.** If your woodwork is smooth, just give it a once-over with 120-grit sandpaper. But if your trim is in rough shape like ours, start with 80-grit sandpaper. Switch to 100 grit for smoothing and blending in the areas with layered paint. Finally, go over all the wood with 120 grit. Buy sandpaper labeled "no-load." No-load sandpaper won't clog as easily and is better for sanding painted surfaces.

NO-LOAD SANDPAPER

2. **Fill holes and dents.** To repair large dents or gouges on edges that are vulnerable to abuse, use hardening-type two-part wood filler. Fill smaller dents and holes with spackling compound. Since spackling compound shrinks as it dries, you'll have to apply a second (and posslbly a third) coat after the previous coat dries. Shine a strong light across the woodwork to highlight depressions and ensure that you don't miss any spots as you're applying the filler. Let the filler dry and sand it smooth.

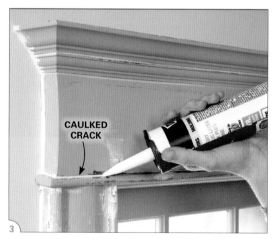

SPACKLING COMPOUND

3. **Caulk for a seamless look.** Here's a step that many beginners don't know about but pros swear by. Caulk every crack or gap, no matter how small. Use latex caulk or a paintable latex/silicone blend. The key is to cut the caulk tube tip very carefully to create a tiny, 1/16-in.-diameter hole. Fill all the small cracks first. Then, if you have wider cracks to fill, recut the caulk tube tip to make a larger hole. Move the caulk gun swiftly along the cracks to avoid an excess buildup of caulk. If necessary, smooth the caulk with your fingertip. Keep a damp rag in your pocket to clean caulk from your finger and to keep the tip of the caulk tube clean. If caulk piles up

CAULKED CRACK

STAIN-BLOCKING PRIMER

4

LATEX PAINT CONDITIONER

5

in the corners, remove the excess with a flexible putty knife.

4. **Spot-prime to avoid blotches.** Brush a stain-sealing primer (B-I-N is one brand) over the areas that you've patched or filled, and over areas where you've sanded down to bare wood. If you have a lot of patches and bare spots, it'll be faster and easier to just prime the entire surface. Also seal discolored areas or marks left by crayons, pens or markers to prevent them from bleeding through the finish coat of paint.

5. **Add an extender to latex paint.** Most pros prefer to use oil-based paint on trim for two reasons: Oil-based paint doesn't dry as fast as water-based paint, leaving more time to brush. And oil-based paint levels out better than most water-based paints, leaving a smoother surface with few visible brush marks. But because water-based paint is more environmentally friendly, less stinky and easier to clean up, it's a better choice for DIYers. You can make water-based paint perform more like oil paint by adding latex paint conditioner (Floetrol is one brand.) Conditioners make the paint flow better and slow down the drying time, allowing you more time to spread the paint without leaving brush marks. Check with the manufacturer of the paint you're using to see if it recommends a particular brand of conditioner. Also, paint from a separate pail. Pour paint about 1-1/2 in. deep into a separate pail. A metal painter's pail or an empty 5-quart ice cream pail works great. Placing a small amount of paint in a pail allows you to easily load the bristles of the brush by dipping them about 1 in. into the paint.

6. **Slap, don't wipe.** Slap the brush gently against each side of the bucket to remove the excess paint. This method of brush loading is best for laying on paint because it keeps the bristles fully loaded with paint.

7. **Cut in edges before you fill the center.** Cutting in is a skill that takes practice to master, but it's worth the effort. To cut in, first load the brush. Then wipe most of the excess paint off by gently scraping the bristles on the edge of the can. Start by pulling the brush along the edge, but keep the bristles about 1/4 in. away from the wall or ceiling to deposit some paint on the wood. Now return with another brushstroke, this time a little closer. Sneaking up to the line like this is easier than trying to get it perfect on the first try. At the end of the stroke, arc the brush away from the cut-in line. Cut in a few feet and then fill the middle using the lay-on, lay-off technique shown in photo 8.

8. **Lay on, lay off.** The biggest mistake beginners make is to work the paint too long after it's applied. Remember, the paint starts to dry as soon as you put it on, and you have to smooth it out before this happens or you'll end up with brushstrokes or worse. So here's the tip: Load your brush. Then quickly unload on the surface with a few back-and-forth brushstrokes. This is called "laying on" the paint. Repeat this until you've covered a few feet of trim with paint. Don't worry about how it looks yet. Now, without reloading the brush, drag the tips of the

6

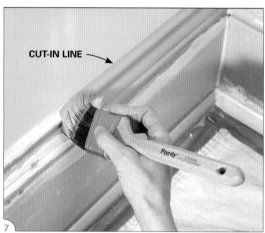

CUT-IN LINE

7

LAYING-OFF STROKE

8

BRUSH MARK

9

10

bristles over the wet paint in one long stroke to "lay off" the paint. Start in the unpainted area and drag into the previously painted trim. Sweep your brush up off the surface at the end of each stroke. Areas wider than your brush will require several parallel laying-off strokes to finish. When you're done laying off a section, move on and repeat the process, always working quickly to avoid brushing over partially dried paint. Try to complete shorter pieces of trim with a continuous laying-off brushstroke.

9. **Don't start a brushstroke on already-smoothed paint.** Setting the paintbrush on an area that's already been smoothed out with laying-off strokes will leave an unsightly mark. Try to start laying-off strokes at the end of a trim piece or board, or in an unpainted area. Brush toward the finished area. Then sweep the brush up and off, like an airplane taking off from a runway, to avoid leaving a mark.

10. **Don't brush across an edge.** Brushing across an edge wipes paint from the bristles and creates a heavy buildup of paint that will run or drip. Avoid this by brushing toward edges whenever possible. If you must start a brushstroke at an edge, align the bristles carefully as if you're cutting in, instead of wiping them against the edge. If you accidentally get a buildup of paint that could cause a run, spread it out right away with a dry paintbrush or wipe it off with a damp rag or your finger.

PROFESSIONAL
COST: $150
(1 window)

YOUR COST: $45

SAVINGS: $105

COMPLEXITY
Simple

TOOLS
Angled brush

Razor scraper

Screwdriver

Bender Paint Pad

MATERIALS
Sandpaper

Painter's tape

Paint

Painting windows

All of the advice for a long-lasting paint job on woodwork also applies to windows, but windows present a few unique challenges. There's the glass to avoid slopping on, as well as all sorts of hardware and weather stripping. Window paint is subjected to large temperature fluctuations and moisture from condensation. And, windows have to move freely when you're all done. Here we'll show you tips on how to get the best paint job on windows with the least amount of time and effort.

pro tips!

➤ Start early in the day. Unless you live in an area free of bugs and criminals, you'll probably want to reinstall your window sashes and possibly close your windows for the night. And you can't really do that with fresh paint. So plan your paint job to allow time for the paint on the sashes to dry before nightfall.

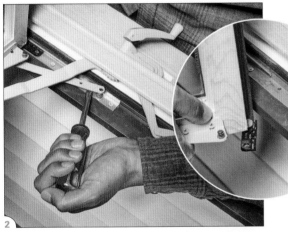

WET GLASS

1

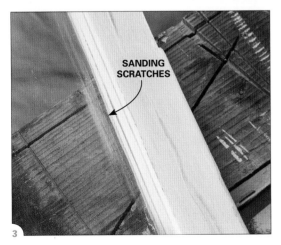

2

SANDING SCRATCHES

3

1. **Clean and scrape before you paint.**
It seems counterintuitive to clean the windows first. But it's a good idea for two reasons. First, your paint job will last longer if the intersection of the glass and wood sash is sealed with paint. You can't get a good seal if the glass is dirty. Second, you'll get a neater paint job if you scrape off previous layers of paint and other crud that may be on the glass.

   Use any window washing solution you prefer and a new, single-edge blade to clean old paint and gunk from the glass. Apply the solution, then scrape, to avoid scraping on dry glass. Never scrape dry glass. Grit pushed by the razor can scratch the window.

2. **Remove the sash.** It's quicker and easier to paint the sash if you take it out of the window frame and rest it on sawhorses or a workbench. The sashes in most modern double-hung, sliding and casement windows are removable. The photos show removing a casement sash. Most newer double-hung windows are removable by pivoting them in and twisting to release them. Old double-hung windows that are held in by wooden stops are more difficult to remove. It may not be worth the effort unless you're a perfectionist.

3. **Sand carefully.** Sandpaper can scratch glass. And it's really easy to accidentally sand the glass where it meets the wood parts of the sash. You can either be extra careful when sanding along the glass, or you can protect the glass with masking tape. Avoid using a power sander along

the edge of the glass because you'd be even more likely to scratch the glass.

4. **Remove the hardware.** This may seem obvious, but if you look around, you'll notice that a lot of painters skip this step. Remove latches and handles from double-hung windows. On casement windows it's much easier to get a neat-looking paint job if you remove the operating hardware from the sash. Just be sure to keep track of the screws and other pieces. Take photos with your phone so you'll know how to reinstall the parts.

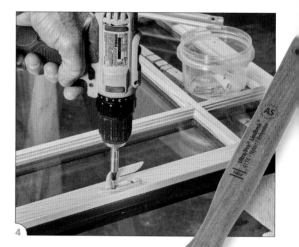

5. **Use an angled brush.** Most of the areas you'll paint on a window aren't very wide, so a narrow 1-1/2-in. angled sash brush will work fine and be easier to control than a wider flat brush. And the angled bristles of a sash brush are specifically designed to neatly apply paint in all of the tight corners and small spaces you'll find on a window. Of course, we always recommend spending a little more money for a top-quality brush and then taking care to clean and store it properly.

6. **Aviod tracks and weather stripping.** Your window tracks and weather strips won't work correctly if they're covered with paint. In some cases, the easiest way to avoid painting these parts is to cover them with masking tape. If there's space, you can also slip a wide putty knife between the wood frame and the track to keep the paint off. If you do slop paint onto these areas, wipe it off right away with a damp rag.

7. **Don't bother to mask the glass.** Covering window glass with masking tape is so time consuming that it's usually quicker

to simply paint neatly along the glass with your brush. If you get a little on the glass, it's easy to scrape it off later with a razor blade. If you'd rather mask the glass, use a masking tape that has edge-seal technology to prevent paint from creeping under the tape.

8. **Move the sash before the paint dries.** This isn't as important if you've removed the sash from the window and waited until it's completely dry to reinstall it. But if you paint your sash in place, avoid a stuck window by opening and closing the window a few times before the paint dries completely. Return to the window about an hour after you've painted it and open and close it to break any paint seal that may have formed. You may even need to do this again the following day just to be sure everything is unstuck.

9. **Paint old windows with a bendable pad.** The upper sash in many old double-hung windows is painted shut, making it difficult to paint the lower rail. You could take time to free up the window, but this can be a big project. Another solution is to buy a Bender Paint Pad from a paint store. Bend the metal to an angle that will allow you to apply paint. Then use a brush to spread some paint on the pad and carefully apply paint to the upper sash. It's tedious but necessary if you don't want to look at ugly drips every time you open your lower sash.

How to use spray paint

The telltale signs of a bad spray-paint job are easy to spot. Stripes of uneven coverage, paint buildup in corners, a stray hair in the finish—and the list goes on. Worst of all is the dreaded run, an obvious sign that the painter applied too heavy a coat. The following tips will help you get a smooth, consistent finish on your next spray-painting project.

1. **Light coats and patience prevent runs.**
The only sure way to avoid runs on a vertical surface is to spray on a light coat and give it a little drying time before the next. That's hard to do if you spray the surfaces in random order, but easy if you have a strategy. Start by coating each vertical surface. Spray lightly to avoid runs. Then hit the horizontal areas before starting the second round. Repeat each round in the same order. That way, each surface will get maximum drying time before you return to it. If any vertical surface still looks wet, stop and remember this: An extra five minutes of drying time now is better than sanding out runs and respraying later.

pro tips!

➤ Don't set your project directly on a workbench or newspaper; the paint will glue it to the work surface. The best way to prop up wood furniture is to drive screws into the legs.

2. **Overlap 50 percent.** If you overlap just a little, you'll get stripes of heavy and light coverage. So instead, aim for 50 percent overlap, with each pass overlapping the previous pass about halfway.

3. **Don't swing an arc.** It's the most natural motion for your arm, but swinging an arc gives you heavy coverage in the middle of the project and light coverage at the ends. So move the can parallel to the surface, concentrating on straight, steady motion.

DO THIS

NOT THIS

4.

5

4. **Get a handle.** If you've ever sprayed a project that required several cans of paint, you already know about finger strain. For less than five bucks, a trigger handle not only prevents the pain but also gives you better control of the can.

5. **Start before; stop after.** Spray nozzles often spit out a few large droplets when you start spraying and again when you stop. To keep sputter spatter off your project, pull the trigger before you're over the target and release the trigger after you're past the edge. Remember: start before; stop after.

6. **Smooth a rough surface.** If you want a smooth finish, pick the right primer. Some are formulated to fill pockmarks and scratches. Plus, they're sandable so you can smooth the surface before top-coating with paint.

7. **Spin and spray.** On some projects, you can walk miles circling the item to spray all the surfaces. Instead, pick up a lazy Susan at a discount store and save some steps.

8. **Two cans are faster and sometimes better.** Spray-painting a big surface isn't just slow; it can also lead to texture trouble. In warm, dry conditions, spray paint dries almost instantly, so very light "overspray" may land on nearby paint that's almost dry. When that happens, you get inconsistencies in the surface texture.

Here's how to get paint onto the project faster and get a consistent finish: Hold a can in each hand. If you move each hand independently, one hand will stray off course. But if you hold the cans together, creating a single spray pattern, it's easy to stay on track. Keep in mind that this trick can lead to drips on vertical surfaces. Make faster passes and try a practice run on a scrap of cardboard.

9. **Plastic paint works!** Conventional spray paints just won't stick to plastic. Now paint manufacturers offer paint just for that application. These paints don't just stick; they fuse with the plastic surface to form a super-strong bond.

SAFETY TIP

This is the warning on a typical spray paint can label: "Repeated or prolonged exposure to these chemicals without the use of a proper respirator can cause permanent brain damage, as well as damage to your lungs."

Less expensive N95 particulate filtering respirators do a great job of filtering out particulate matter. But they don't adsorb toxic chemical vapors. To do that, you need activated carbon. The bottom line is, any carbon filter respirator rated for solvents and paint is better than a cheap particulate respirator. To save money over the long run, buy a respirator that accepts replaceable filter cartridges and keep a few extras on hand.

8 tips for a neater paint job

The first thing to do as you prepare to paint is move furnishings for easy access to the walls and ceiling. Cramped working conditions lead to messy accidents. Every painter has stepped in a paint pan or kicked over a pail while squeezing a ladder past the couch. If you can't move furniture and other big stuff completely out of the room, stack it up. Set upholstered chairs upside down on the sofa. Cover the dining room table-top with cardboard so you can set chairs on top of it. But don't let your stack become an obstacle.

Get out your ladder and roller and make a dry run to be sure you can easily reach all parts of the ceiling. In some cases, two smaller stacks with space for a ladder between them is better than one. Maintain a generous workspace of at least 3 ft. between the stack and the walls. Cover your furniture stack with plastic. Even if you're careful, some drips and splatters are likely. A couple of bands of duct tape will keep the plastic in place and hold the stack together if you bump into it.

Here are more ways to paint neatly

1. **Cover the carpet with canvas drops.** Canvas dropcloths are absolutely the best coverings for carpet. They're easy to spread out, and unlike plastic, they stay put without tape. And they won't cause your ladder to slip-slide on carpet. Just bunch them up a bit along walls and they'll stay where you want them. Normal drips and splatter won't soak through canvas, but heavy spills will. Pick up the dropcloths and scoop up spills with a broad putty knife or dustpan.

    These dropcloths aren't cheap, but you don't have to cover the entire floor. Our favorite drop is a long, narrow "runner" that you can drag around the room as you go. A runner is also perfect for carpeted stairs; just fasten it to the steps with small nails so you don't trip.

2. **Protect hard floors with rosin paper.** Both canvas and plastic dropcloths are slippery when laid over wood, vinyl and tile. For protection that stays put on hard surfaces, you can't beat rosin paper. Just tape sheets of it together and then tape the perimeter to the floor. Be sure to clean wood floors thoroughly before laying down the paper; grit trapped underneath can lead to scratches. A single layer will protect against paint drips, but wipe up any spills before they can soak through.

3. **Remove cover plates, then tape over switches and outlets.** Paint slopped on electrical cover plates, switches and outlets looks tacky. Don't try to paint around them. Removing cover plates takes just a few seconds and makes for a faster, neater job. Grab a small bucket to hold all the odds and ends you'll take off

CAUTION
Turn off the power to the room before removing cover plates. With the plates removed, live terminals inside the box are exposed.

the walls. Unscrew cover plates and then shield each switch or outlet with 2-in. wide masking tape. Also remove curtain hardware, picture hooks, grilles that cover duct openings and anything else that might get in your way. The thermostat is one exception—it's easier to wrap it with masking tape than to remove and reinstall it.

4. **Shelter baseboard with overhanging tape.** Don't waste time by completely covering baseboard with several strips of tape. A single overhanging strip of wide tape will catch roller splatters just as the roof overhang on your house keeps rain off the siding. Use 1-1/2 in. tape for narrow baseboard, 2-in. tape for wider baseboard. Tape won't stay stuck to dusty surfaces, so wipe down all your trim before masking. To minimize paint seepage under the tape, press the tape down hard by running a flexible putty knife over it.

5. **Use wide tape and plastic to protect doors and windows.** Paint rollers throw off a mist of paint that speckles everything below. Here's the quickest way to protect doors and windows: When you tape around door and window trim to protect the woodwork, use tape that's wide enough to project at least 1/2 in. from the trim. That way, you can stick light plastic to the protruding tape—there's no need to tape the perimeter of the plastic separately. For doors, slit the plastic with a utility knife so you can walk through.

6. **Mask off sensitive wiring and tuck it in the box.** A little paint in the wrong place can cripple the connections that serve your TV or computer. Slip the plate

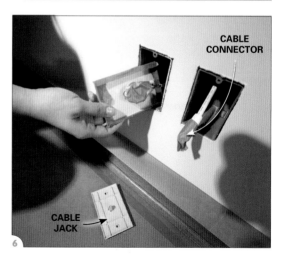

CABLE CONNECTOR

CABLE JACK

TEMPORARY HANGING WIRE ←

7

into the junction box. Disconnect coaxial cable from its plate and tape the cable's connector.

7. **Hang and bag light fixtures.** Painting a ceiling is a cinch (see p. 102)—except for the light fixture. Here's how to get it out of your way: First remove any glass parts, including the bulbs (make sure the power is off). Unfasten the fixture, usually by removing a couple of screws. Then hook one end of a wire through the fixture and the other to the junction box. Make sure your hanger wire—not the electrical wire—supports the fixture. Then slip a plastic bag over the fixture. Dealing with chandeliers and pendants is even easier. The decorative plate at the ceiling is usually held up by a ring nut. Just unscrew the nut and the plate will slide down over the chain or tube. There's no need to support the fixture with wire.

pro tips!

➤ **Fast blotting will save your carpet.** Spilling on carpet may seem like the ultimate painting disaster, but it doesn't have to leave a permanent stain. The keys to complete stain removal are speed and lots of water. Latex paint dries fast and seconds count. Don't go for the water bucket yourself. Shout for someone else to bring it. Immediately scoop up the spill with a wide putty knife, dustpan or whatever is handy. Don't wipe up the spill; you'll just force the paint deeper into the carpet. Then start to blot the paint with a wet (not just damp) rag. Keep the paint wet. Continue blotting, refill the bucket with clean water and blot some more until the paint is no longer visible. When you're done, set up a fan to dry out the soaked carpet. For small drips or splatters, use the opposite approach. Just let the paint dry. Tiny drops of paint will sit on the carpet's surface. Just be careful not to step on them. After they dry, trim them off with scissors.

Chapter 5

Store and Organize

Tips for a tidy garage

The garage tends to be a dumping ground for everything from lawn chairs to sports gear and oversized grocery items. When you start parking on the street because your car no longer fits, it's time to fight back!

Most garage storage projects are simple, inexpensive and highly functional. Here we've gathered our best storage projects, tricks and tips that are well suited to beginner-level DIYers. Check out the space-saving overhead storage projects, the nifty cabinet for car-care tools and supplies, and all of the great tips for storing sports gear.

In one weekend, you can organize your garage and start parking inside once again!

Dustpan caddy

Keep a dustpan handy with an "unbreakable" wall file folder. Attach the file folder to the garbage can with 8-32 x 3/4-in. machine bolts and nuts. Position the screw heads inside the garbage can so the bag doesn't snag on the end of the bolt.

Storage tubes

Cardboard concrete-forming tubes are inexpensive and provide a great place to store baseball bats, long-handled tools and rolls of just about anything. Rest the tubes on a piece of 2x4 to keep them high and dry. Secure each tube to a garage stud with a plumbing strap.

WOOD BLOCK

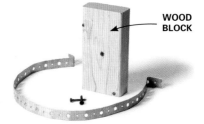

WOOD BLOCK

Double-duty shelf brackets

Shelf brackets designed to support clothes hanger rods aren't just for closets. The rod-holding hook on these brackets comes in handy in the garage and workshop too. You can bend the hook to suit long tools or cords. Inexpensive closet brackets are sold at home centers and hardware stores.

Closet pole and shelf brackets can also keep your bikes up and out of the way of car doors and bumpers. Just screw the brackets to the wall studs. Line the pole carriage with self-stick hook-and-loop strips so it won't scratch your bike frame.

SELF-STICK HOOK-AND-LOOP

CLOSET POLE AND SHELF BRACKET

Garage ceiling track storage

If you store stuff in big plastic storage bins and you need a place to put them, how about the garage ceiling? Screw 2x2s to the ceiling framing with 3-1/2-in. screws spaced every 2 ft. Use the bins as a guide for spacing the 2x2s. The lips on the bins should just brush against the 2x2s when you're sliding the bins into place. Then center and screw 1x4s to the 2x2s with 2-in. screws. The garage ceiling is a perfect place to store light- and medium-weight seasonal items like holiday decorations and camping gear.

2" SCREW

3-1/2" SCREW

2x2

1x4

Easy lawn chair storage

Here's how to store lawn and folding chairs so they're out of your way. Take two pieces of 1x4 lumber (any scrap lumber will do) and create some simple, cheap and useful brackets on the wall. Cut each board 7-3/4 in. long with a 30-degree angle on both ends. Fasten pairs of these brackets with three 2-in. screws to the side of the exposed wall studs, directly across from each other, and you've got a perfect place to hang your chairs.

Save your lawn products

Leave a bag of fertilizer or weed killer open for long and it'll soak up moisture from the air and won't go through a spreader. Even grass seed could use an extra layer of protection from a moisture-wicking concrete floor. Place opened bags of lawn products in large resealable plastic bags. The products will be free of clumps or pests when you need them.

GIANT RESEALABLE PLASTIC BAG

Up-and-away storage

The perfect place to store small quantities of long, narrow offcuts and moldings is right over your head. Build this set of overhead storage racks either in high basement ceilings or in the open trusses in the garage. Use 2x6s for the vertical hangers and doubled-up 3/4-in. plywood for the lower angled supports. Secure each 2x6 into the framing with two 5/16 x 3-in. lag screws. Screw each hanger into the 2x6 with two offset 5/16 x 3-in. lag screws. The angle on the supports keeps stuff from sliding off.

Ski and pole organizer

Keep your skis up and easy to find with this simple 2x4 rack. Drill 3/4-in.-diameter holes spaced 3/4 in. apart. Glue 4-1/2-in. lengths of 3/4-in. dowel into the holes and then mount the 2x4 to the wall studs. Space the groupings about 8 in. apart to make room for ski bindings. Now you'll spend less time looking for your skis and more time on the trails.

Upside-down shelves!

Here's some neat and fast storage for your garage's upper regions. Bolt together a set of inexpensive metal shelves and attach them upside down to the ceiling joists with lag bolts. The spacing between shelves is completely adjustable. Hang the shelves so they're easy to reach, or set them high so you won't bonk your head. Trim the shelf posts to just the right height with tin snips.

Under-joist shelf

Create extra storage space by screwing wire closet shelving to joists in your garage or basement. Wire shelving is see-through, so you can easily tell what's up there.

Movable bike rack

Tired of that darn bike hanging in your way? Build this movable bike rack from a 2x4 and a pair of bicycle hooks. Cut four 3-1/2-in. blocks, stack two on top of each other, and screw them together. Now screw them on the end of a 4-ft. 2x4 and repeat the process for the other side. Drill a hole in the middle of the stacked blocks and screw in the bicycle hooks. Lay the rack across your garage ceiling trusses, and hang your bike from the hooks. When you need to get behind the bike, simply slide the entire rack out of the way.

Stay-put balls

Keep sport balls off the floor and out of the way by resting them in flowerpot drip saucers. Screw the saucers down to an inexpensive shelving unit. The balls will stay put.

Simple storage rack

Use this storage rack for lumber and other long stuff. Simply drill a line of 3/4-in. holes about 1-1/2 in. deep in adjacent studs, angling the holes slightly downward. Then insert 15-in.-long sections of 1/2-in. galvanized pipe. Keep the lowest pipes at least 6 ft. above the floor so you won't crack your skull on them.

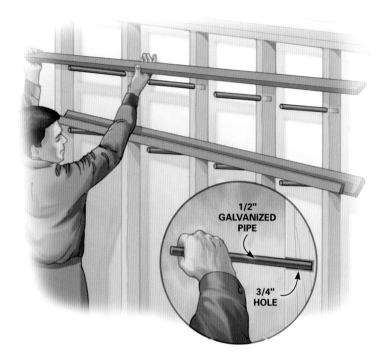

**1/2"
GALVANIZED
PIPE**

**3/4"
HOLE**

Fishing rod holder

Here's an easy way to store fishing rods so they're out of the way. Use two pieces of 1/4-in. or thicker plywood, 8 in. wide or so. Drill holes in one piece, and slots in the other. Screw them to your garage rafters.

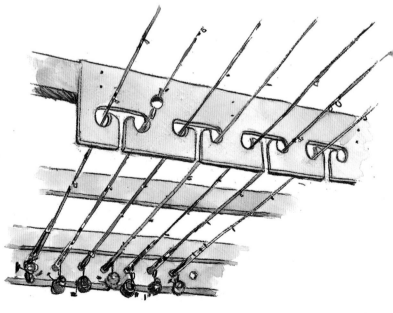

Inexpensive storage cylinders

Build cheap storage cylinders from PVC pipe, end caps, female adapters and cleanout plugs. Parts are available in an assortment of diameters at any hardware store or home center. Cut the pipe to length with a handsaw or chop saw. Glue an end cap to one end and a female adapter to the other pipe end with PVC cement. Twist in a threaded cleanout plug for a cap. If sealing isn't important, you can drill holes in the pipe to decrease the cylinder's weight. Use the cylinders to store and protect fishing rods, drill bits, cross-country skis, blueprints or anything long and skinny.

Hang-it-all hooks

Those plastic hooks that plumbers use to support pipes make convenient hangers for just about anything. They're strong, cheap and come in a range of sizes. Find them in the plumbing aisle at home centers and hardware stores.

FEMALE ADAPTER

CLEANOUT PLUG

Tidy up your kitchen

One of the hardest-working and most public spaces inside your home is the kitchen. And with all of that activity, the kitchen is also one of the hardest spaces to keep organized. Cooking and baking equipment and utensils, groceries of all types and clean and dirty dishes all need their own space, and that can't always be the countertop!

Here you'll find 16 simple, inexpensive ways to tidy up your busy kitchen. Each project is beginner-friendly and can be completed in just a few hours.

Wine glass molding

T-molding designed for wood floor transitions makes a perfect rack for stemware. Just cut it to length, predrill screw holes and screw it to the underside of a shelf. For a neater look, use brass screws and finish washers. Prefinished T-molding is available wherever wood flooring is sold.

T-MOLDING

FINISH WASHER

Cutting board rack

You can make this nifty rack for just a few dollars and mount it inside a cabinet door to stash your cutting boards out of sight. It goes together in a snap since it only requires a 6-ft. 1x2 and two L-brackets. Measure between the door stiles to get the maximum width of your rack. Make sure the rack will be wide enough for your cutting board. You'll also need to mount the rack low enough so it doesn't bump into a cabinet shelf when the door closes. Cut the bottom and face rails to match the space between the cabinet door stiles.

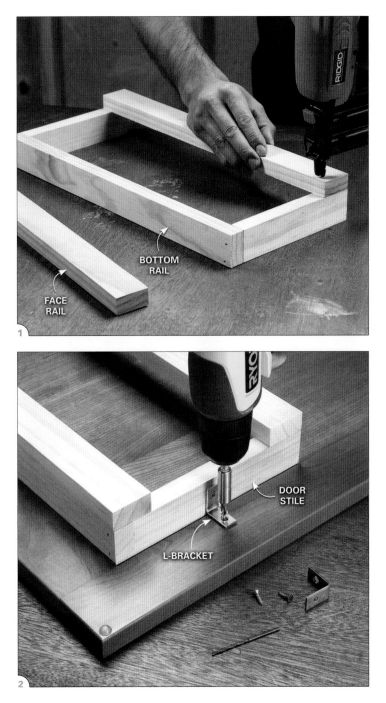

FACE RAIL

BOTTOM RAIL

DOOR STILE

L-BRACKET

1. Cut the sides 7-1/4 in. long. Nail the sides to the base. Then nail the two face pieces at the top and bottom to complete the rack.

2. The easiest way to mount the rack is to take the cabinet door off its hinges and lay it down. Predrill the screw holes for the L-brackets and mount the rack to the cabinet door using a 1-in. L-bracket centered on each side of the rack.

Adjustable spice shelf

This in-cabinet spice shelf puts small containers at eye level and still leaves room in the cabinet for tall items. You'll need a 4-ft. 1x3 for the top shelf and a 4-ft. 1x2 for the bottom ledger. You can find shelf pegs at home centers in two sizes, 1/4 in. and 3/16 in., so measure the holes in your cabinet before you shop. The secret is to assemble the shelf outside the cabinet and then set it on the shelf pegs.

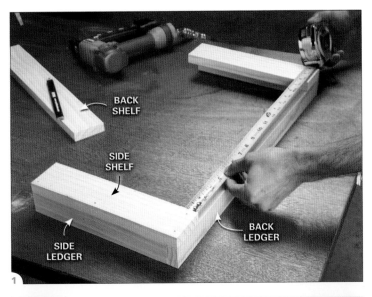

1. Measure the sides and back of your cabinet and cut your shelf and ledger pieces. Subtract 1/8 in. from all sides so you can fit the unit into the cabinet. Attach the sides to the back of the bottom ledger and put two nails into each butt joint. Then nail the top shelf sides into place and pin the shelf back at the corners to hold it flush.

2. To install the shelf unit, carefully fit one end of the "U" into the cabinet, holding it higher at one end, and shimmy it down until it sits firmly on top of the shelf pegs. Shift the pegs up or down to adjust the shelf height. Spray a quick coat of lacquer on the shelf before installing it.

Cabinet door message board

A sheet of metal and a whiteboard can turn any cabinet door into a convenient message center. You'll find 2- x 2-ft. lengths of plastic-coated hardboard (sometimes called dry-erase board) and sheet metal at a hardware store or home center. Larger hardware stores will cut the sheet metal to your specifications. Be sure to get steel instead of aluminum so magnets will stick.

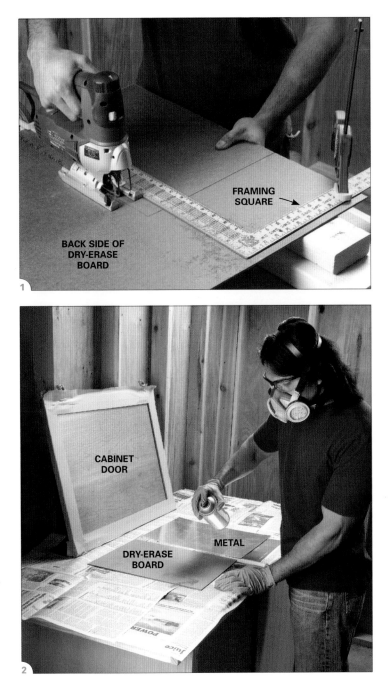

BACK SIDE OF DRY-ERASE BOARD

FRAMING SQUARE →

CABINET DOOR

METAL

DRY-ERASE BOARD

1. If you cut the metal yourself, wear gloves to protect your hands and use tin snips carefully. Use a metal file to smooth any ragged edges. If you don't have a table saw to cut the whiteboard, flip it over, mark your measurements and use a jigsaw to cut it from the back to prevent chipping or splintering. To get a straight cut, use a framing square as a guide.

2. To mount the metal sheet and whiteboard to the inside of the door, take the door off its hinges, lay it flat and carefully mask off the area where you want to spray the adhesive. Follow the directions on the can to apply the adhesive to the door, metal and whiteboard. Mount the pieces, press firmly and let dry.

Cookware organizer

Most kitchen base cabinets lack vertical storage space for big, flat cookware like cookie sheets and pizza pans. To provide it, just remove the lower shelf, cut a vertical panel of plywood and fasten it at the cabinet bottom with furniture braces and at the top with a strip of wood. Drill holes for the adjusting pins to match the original locations and trim the shelf to length.

Measuring cup hang-up

Free up drawer space by hanging measuring cups inside a kitchen cabinet. Position and mount a wood strip so that the cups will hang between the shelves and allow the door to close completely. Mount a second strip for your measuring spoons, then screw in cup hooks on both strips.

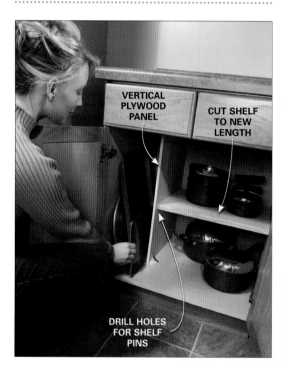

VERTICAL PLYWOOD PANEL

CUT SHELF TO NEW LENGTH

DRILL HOLES FOR SHELF PINS

Plastic bag dispenser

Make it easy to stow and reuse plastic bags with a dispenser made from a discarded 2-liter soda bottle. Cut off the top and bottom with a razor knife. Trim any jagged edges so you don't tear the bags when you pull them out, then screw the dispenser to a cabinet door or closet wall (or attach with hook-and-loop tape).

Racks for canned goods

Use those leftover closet racks as cabinet organizers. Trim the racks to length with a hacksaw and then mount screws to the back side of the face frame to hold the racks in place. The back side of the rack simply rests against the back of the cabinet. Now you can easily find your soup and check the rest of your inventory at a glance.

CLOSET ORGANIZER RACKS

ATTACH SCREWS TO BACK SIDE OF FACE FRAME

Spice drawer

If your spices are jammed into a drawer with only the tops visible, this nifty rack that slips neatly into the drawer will solve the problem. And it only takes an hour to build. Make it with scraps of 1/4-in. and 1/2-in. plywood.

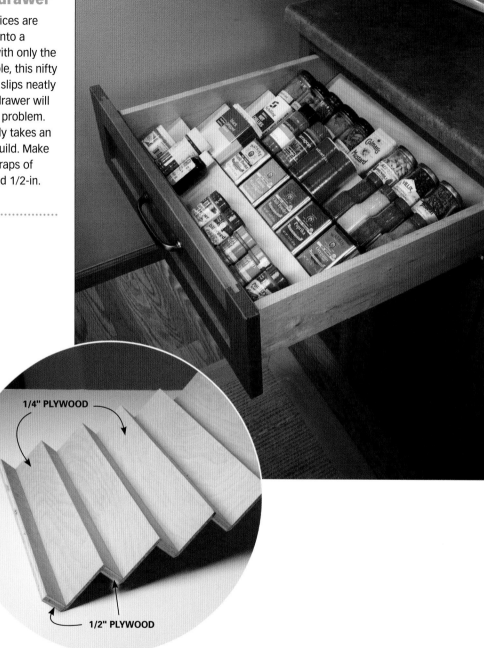

1/4" PLYWOOD

1/2" PLYWOOD

Spice mini-shelf

Small spice containers use shelf space inefficiently and are difficult to find when surrounded by taller bottles and items. Use a small spring-tension curtain rod as a simple shelf. It's easy to install and strong enough to support the spices.

Quick bathroom helpers

Have you ever heard anyone say that their bathroom was plenty big and they didn't need any more storage space?

Bathrooms are notorious for being cramped and not having enough room to store towels, toiletries, hair products and all of the other stuff each family member needs. Here are five of our favorite DIY ways to take control of the bathroom.

PVC curling iron holsters

Use hook-and-loop tape to attach 5-in. lengths of 2-in.-diameter PVC pipe to the vanity door to hold curling irons. You can do the same thing with 3-in. pieces of 1-1/2-in.-diameter pipe to hold the cords. Just measure your curling irons to see how long your holsters need to be. Always let curling irons cool before you stow them away.

Toilet paper shelf

Buy an inexpensive, deep shadow box picture frame at a craft store. Hang it around your toilet paper holder. Now you've got two convenient shelves for small items.

1-1/2" PVC   2" PVC

Under-sink organizer

To keep bottles from tipping over under your bathroom sink, make this organizer from scraps of 3-in. PVC pipe. Cut the pipe into short lengths with a hacksaw and then glue them to 1/2-in. plywood with polyurethane construction adhesive. Space the pipe pieces to accommodate liquid soaps, shampoos and other bottles and leave spaces between the pipe sections for odd-shaped spray bottles.

His-and-hers shower shelves

If you need more than shampoo and a bar of soap in the shower, here's how to provide space for all your vital beauty potions: Get a couple of those shelves that are designed to hang from a shower arm and hang them on cabinet knobs. Use 8-32 hanger screws to screw the knobs into studs or drywall anchors.

Magnetic toothbrush holder

The problem: Battery-powered toothbrushes don't fit in toothbrush holders and end up lying on a wet, messy countertop.

The solution: Mount neodymium ("rare earth") magnets on a Corian mounting strip with Super Glue. Glue the strip to the wall with Super Glue or silicone caulk.

Tools and materials: To make the mounting strip, cut a Corian threshold (available at tile stores) with a miter saw or jigsaw. Neodymium magnets are available from kjmagnetics.com and other Internet suppliers. Shown here are 1/2-in. x 2-in. x 1/8-in. magnets (No. BY082). You can double them up if you need more holding power.

Note: Neodymium magnets are incredibly strong but break if handled roughly. Order several more than you need—shipping is expensive. Also, don't handle neodymium magnets if you wear a pacemaker, and never leave them next to your computer. For more safety information, see the "Neo Mag Safety" link at kjmagnetics.com.

....

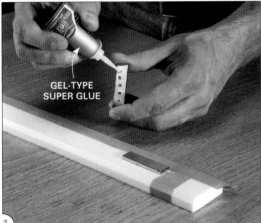

GEL-TYPE
SUPER GLUE

1. Mark the position of the magnets and glue them on the mounting strip, orienting the magnets so they attract each other.

2. Glue the mounting strip to the wall with Super Glue, hot-melt glue or silicone caulk.

12"

4-1/2"
MINIMUM

#4 x 3/8"
SCREW

Make any toothbrush stick
Battery-powered toothbrushes have hidden steel parts that stick to magnets. Mount standard toothbrushes by adding a tiny screw or metal washer to the back.

Tips for tidy closets

Never underestimate the power of a well-organized closet!

By customizing your closets with shelves, rods and hooks that work with your clothes, linens and other household items, you'll be able to find what you want when you want it. Here are seven simple solutions you can use to conquer closet chaos once and for all.

Closet glove rack

If you don't have radiators, finding a good spot to dry wet hats and mittens can be tough. Tossing them into a plastic bin gets them out of the way, but they never dry and it's no fun putting on damp mittens in the morning. This simple back-of-the-door glove and cap rack allows wet things to dry and keeps easily misplaced items organized. Just string clothespins on aluminum wire (it won't rust) and stretch it between screw eyes on the back of a closet door. This also works great out in the garage for drying garden and work gloves.

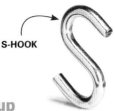

S-HOOK

S-hook hang-up

Turn any closet into a useful hang-up storage space by adding S-hooks to wire shelving. This provides tidy storage for mops, brooms and other cleaning tools.

18-GAUGE ALUMINUM WIRE

SCREW EYE

Two-story closet shelves

There's a lot of space above the shelf in most closets. Even though it's a little hard to reach, it's a great place to store seldom-used items. Make use of this wasted space by adding a second shelf above the existing one. Buy enough closet shelving material to match the length of the existing shelf plus enough for two end supports and middle supports over each bracket. Twelve-inch-wide shelving is available in various lengths and finishes at home centers and lumberyards. These supports were cut at 16 in. long, but you can place the second shelf at whatever height you like. Screw the end supports to the walls at each end. Use drywall anchors if you can't hit a stud. Then mark the position of the middle supports onto the top and bottom shelves with a square and drill 5/32-in. clearance holes through the shelves. Drive 1-5/8-in. screws through the shelf into the supports.

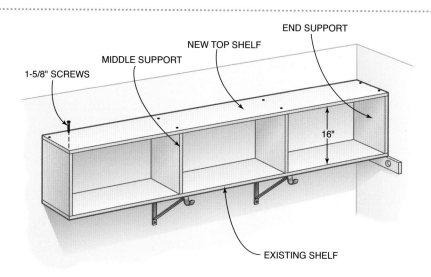

END SUPPORT

NEW TOP SHELF

MIDDLE SUPPORT

1-5/8" SCREWS

16"

EXISTING SHELF

Temporary valet rod

When you need temporary clothes-hanging space around the house, keep an extra shower tension bar handy. Put it between the jambs in the laundry room door on heavy laundry days. Or, use it in the bedroom closet to pack for trips or stick it in the closet opening in the guest room/den so overnight guests can hang up their clothes. It's a quick and easy way to gain an extra closet!

SHOWER TENSION BAR

Accessory clip-up

Create the perfect hangers for soft items like hats and gloves using a length of metal or plastic chain and binder clips. Squeeze the metal handles to free them from the clips, slip them through the chain links, then reattach the clips. You'll have a neat hangout for all your winter gear.

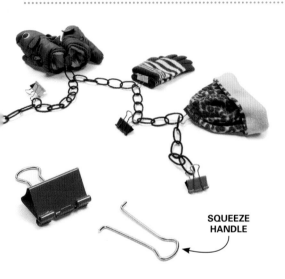

SQUEEZE HANDLE

Belts & other hang-ups

Where do you store your belts? (A) on the floor, (B) over a chair, (C) stuffed in a drawer or (D) all of the above? Well, you can now choose (E)—on an inexpensive and easy-to-make belt holder. All you need is a wooden hanger and some cup hooks. If some of your belts have unusually thick buckles, just widen the cup hook slightly with needle-nose pliers. This is a great way to hang small handbags, too.

CUP HOOK

Closet nook shelves

Salvage the hidden space at the recessed ends of your closets by adding a set of shelves. Wire shelves are available in a variety of widths. Measure the width and depth of the space. Then choose the correct shelving and ask the salesperson to cut the shelves to length for you or cut them yourself with a hacksaw. Subtract 3/8 in. from the actual width to determine the shelf length. Buy a pair of end mounting brackets and a pair of plastic clips for each shelf.

SAVINGS: $50

COMPLEXITY
Simple

TOOLS
Drill

Stud finder

Laser level

Regular level

MATERIALS
Figure-eight
fasteners

Screws

Masking tape

Snaptoggle anchors

Hollow-wall anchors

How to install shelves

From leveling to anchoring, here are 10 tips to make sure your next shelf-hanging project is quick, easy and super-strong.

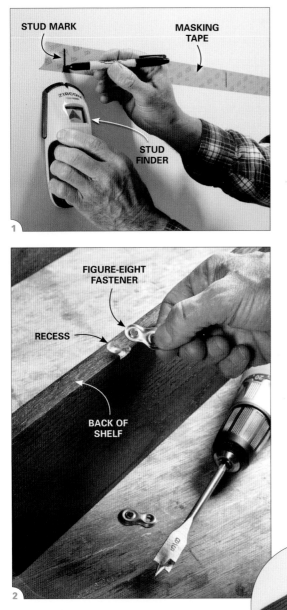

STUD MARK

MASKING TAPE

STUD FINDER

FIGURE-EIGHT FASTENER

RECESS

BACK OF SHELF

1. **Mark the tape, not the wall.** The first step in any shelf-hanging project is to locate the studs so you can anchor the shelf to the studs if possible. Here's a tip that allows you to make marks that are clearly visible without the need to repaint the wall.

   Use a level and draw a very light pencil line where you want the top of the shelf to be. The shelf will hide the line. Apply a strip of masking tape above the line. Use "delicate surface" masking tape to avoid any possibility of messing up the paint. Locate the studs and mark the centers on the tape. Electronic stud finders are the go-to tool for this task. Now you can plan your shelf-mounting project to hit as many studs as possible and use the tape as a guide for leveling and attaching the shelf.

2. **Figure-eights simplify the job.** These nifty little fasteners are actually designed to attach table and desktops to aprons (the vertical skirt around the perimeter of a table), but they're also a handy solution for hanging shelves.

   The only caveat is that the top of the figure-eight shows above the surface of the shelf, so it may be visible if you hang the shelf low. Position the figure-eights where there are studs, if possible. You can use good-quality hollow-wall anchors if the studs don't line up with the figure-eights.

Drill a recess for the figure-eight. Use a spade bit or Forstner bit to drill a slight recess in the back of the shelf to accommodate the thickness of the figure-eight. Then chisel out the remaining wood until the figure-eight sits flush to the shelf. Attach the figure-eight with a screw.

Simply screw it on. Mount the shelf by driving screws through the figure-eights either into hollow-wall anchors or into studs.

3. **Dead-on leveling with a laser.** Got a lot of shelves to level? A laser level is the perfect tool. We're using a self-leveling laser, but any laser that projects a horizontal level line will work. The tip is that you don't have to mess with getting the laser line at the height of your shelf. Just project it anywhere on the wall, and use it as a reference by measuring up from the line. This is especially handy if you're mounting several shelves at different heights, since you never need to reposition the laser.

SHELF LEVEL

LASER LINE

4. **Super-sturdy closet shelves.** Here's a fast, strong and easy way to install closet shelves. Paint a 1x4 to match your shelf. Then draw a level line and locate the studs or use the masking tape trick in Photo 1. Nail the 1x4 to the studs with 8d finish nails. Run the strip across the back and ends of the closet. Then put blocks in the locations where you want brackets. Now you have solid wood to attach the brackets and the closet

HOOK STRIP

KEYHOLE LOCATIONS

MASKING TAPE

KEYHOLE HANGER

5

Mark; don't measure. Place a strip of masking tape on one edge of your level and mark the center of each keyhole on the tape.

Transfer to the wall. Hold the level against the wall at the height you want the shelf. Remember that the top of the shelf will be above your marks. Adjust the level until the bubble is centered, and mark the keyhole locations on the wall. Then install anchors or drive the screws into the studs and hang the shelf.

pole sockets to. And the back of the shelf is fully supported to prevent sagging.

5. **The key to keyholes.** Keyhole slots on the back of shelves are a common way to hang shelves or brackets on hidden screws, but you have to get the screws perfectly aligned or you'll have all kinds of trouble. Here's one foolproof method for transferring a pair of keyhole locations to the wall for perfect screw placement. If you're lucky, you may be able to line up the screw locations with studs. Otherwise, use this method to mark the center of the hollow-wall anchors you'll need.

6. **Ditch those old-school toggle bolts.** Of course it's always best to fasten heavy shelves to studs, but if you can't, there's an anchor that's almost as good. If you've used standard toggle bolts,

you know they hold well. But they're a hassle to work with, and they leave an oversize hole that may show. And if you ever need to take the shelf down to paint, the toggle falls into the wall and you have to repeat the whole tedious

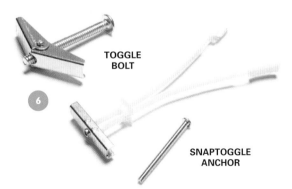

TOGGLE BOLT

6

SNAPTOGGLE ANCHOR

process when you reinstall the shelf. Snaptoggle anchors solve these problems. After installing the toggle according to the instructions, you'll have a threaded opening in the wall ready to receive the included bolt. You can simply screw the shelf to the captured toggle. And you can remove the bolt and the toggle will stay put, ready for you to reinstall the shelf. You'll find Snaptoggle anchors in hardware stores and home centers alongside the other wall anchors.

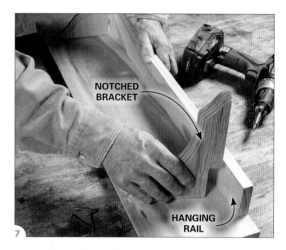

NOTCHED BRACKET

HANGING RAIL

7

7. **Build in a hanging rail.** Whether you're building a shelf or modifying a store-bought unit, including a hanging rail is a great way to add strength and allow for more flexible positioning while anchoring to studs. The rail strengthens the shelf and lets you anchor the shelf by driving screws anywhere along the length of the rail. If the shelf isn't too heavy, you can hang it with finish-head screws that are easy to hide with wood putty. For heavier shelves, drill recesses for wood plugs to hide the screws.

8. **Self-plumbing standards.** The next time you install metal shelf standards, remember this tip. Rather than use a level to plumb the standards before you attach them, simply hang them loosely from the top with one of the screws and let gravity do the work. The standard will hang plumb, and all you have to do is press it to the wall and drive in the remaining screws. If you're using hollow-wall anchors, hang the standard from the top screw and use an awl to mark the screw locations. Then take the standard down and install the anchors.

LOOSE SCREW

SHELF STANDARD

8

9. **Throw away the free anchors.** Most of the hollow-wall anchors included with shelves or shelf brackets aren't worth using. If you can't attach your shelf to studs and must use hollow-wall anchors, make sure to choose one that will support your shelf in the long run. For light-duty shelves, we like the type of anchor shown here. You'll find them at any hardware store or home center. Make sure you know how thick your dry-wall or plaster is before you head to the store, though. Then match the anchor to the wall thickness. To install the anchors, check the instructions and drill the right size hole. Then fold the wings so the anchor will fit and press it into the hole. You may have to tap it with a hammer until it's fully seated. Finish by pressing the included red tool through the hole to expand the wings behind the drywall or plaster. And make sure to use the screws included with the anchors, or ones that are the same diameter.

10. **French cleats for fast, solid hanging.** Pairs of beveled strips that interlock to support shelves, cabinets or pictures are called French cleats. They're great for hanging any shelf or cabinet and have a few advantages in certain situations. First, the cleats work well for heavy cabinets because you can easily mount the wall cleat and then simply lift the cabinet and "hook" it on. There's no need to support a heavy cabinet tempo-rarily while you drive screws to anchor it. Another common use for French cleats is to create a flexible system of shelves or cabinets. You can screw one or more lengths of wall cleats across the entire wall, and then easily relocate shelves, or add more shelves at a later date. Make cleats by ripping strips of 3/4-in. plywood with a 45-degree bevel on one edge. Screw one strip to the wall and the other to the back of the shelf or cabinet.

SHELF CLEAT

WALL CLEAT

10

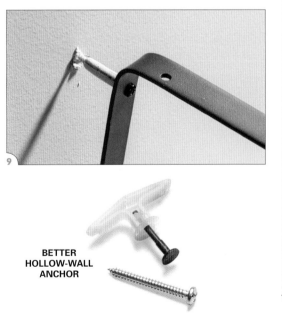

9

BETTER
HOLLOW-WALL
ANCHOR

Projects Any DIYer Can Do

Get rid of mice

PROFESSIONAL
COST: $300

YOUR COST: $25

SAVINGS: $275

COMPLEXITY
Simple

MATERIALS
Snap-style mouse traps

Peanut butter

Weather stripping

Spray foam insulation or other material to plug exterior holes

Most people don't relish killing animals—even mice. If you have a mouse problem, we recommend trapping. Here are our thoughts on the alternatives.

1. **Live traps.** Mice, by nature, build nests and store food. So you trap them this fall and let them go outside where they start their life anew, right? Well, that's not how it works. They have no food stored away and no nest to live in, and they'll most likely die of starvation and/or exposure.

2. **Poison.** Most poisons are ingested and cause severe dehydration or blood coagulation. It's not a painless death.

3. **Live with the disease-carrying creatures.** As they run around your floors, countertops, plates with leftovers and your pet's food dishes, they're leaving a trail of waste behind them and you don't want that.

4. **Sticky mouse traps.** So then what? They're not dead and you have to either kill them with your shoe or throw them into the trash where they'll die a slow, miserable death from thirst.

All this mouse-killing business isn't for the faint-of-heart. Sometimes, but not too often, mice don't get killed right away. And sometimes they suffer. But if you have a mouse problem and ignore it, you're putting your family's health at risk, so here's what you can do.

1. **Buy and set lots of traps.** Anywhere you see mouse droppings is a good place to set traps. And the more traps you set, the more mice you'll catch—period. So don't think you'll place a few traps around the house and take care of your mouse problem. Bait and set the traps at night because that's when the mice are out looking for food.

2. **Peanut butter is the best bait.** Many baits work well, but good old peanut butter is our favorite. (By the way, cheese is one of the least effective.) Here's a tip. Mark the top of the peanut butter bait jar and let your family know what it's for. Think about it: You're baiting the traps with peanut butter and then in the morning Junior might be spreading his toast with contaminated peanut butter. If it makes you less squeamish, use plastic knives and throw them away when you're through rebaiting and resetting traps. Better yet, keep the bait jar out of the kitchen.

3. **Pet food is a problem—and an opportunity.** At night, set traps near your pet's food dishes. Mice are likely to be attracted to the pet food so your traps will be perfectly placed. Keep your pets out of the area after you've set the traps.

4. **Look for the pathways.** A mouse is like Tarzan when it comes to climbing. In fact, a mouse can jump up to 8 in. and climb up electrical cords to get to other places. So if you find droppings in high places, look low and put your traps there.

5. **Under cabinets.** The spaces under cabinets are like a freeway for mice. Pull out your bottom drawers and look for droppings. Put traps down there on the floor, replace the drawers and check them every morning.

6. **Look for wall penetrations.** Mice love to live inside walls where they're safe and warm. Look around to see where plumbing or anything else penetrates drywall or plaster and put traps just below it. That's where they'll come in at night looking for food.

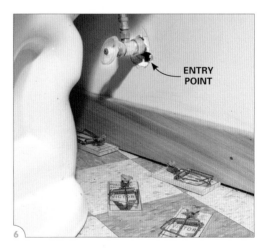

ENTRY POINT

7. **Look for feeding areas.** Just like pet dishes, there are other sources of food that'll attract mice. The stovetop, under the toaster, behind the breadbox—food bits and crumbs in these areas attract mice.

8. **Place traps next to vertical surfaces.** Mice are prey after all, so they're born scared. That means that they're terrified to be out in the open and prefer traveling close to walls. Once again, the more traps the better, especially in areas where you know mice are hanging out, usually where there's food.

9. **Keep 'em out!** When the temperature starts dropping, mice are looking for a warm, dry place with food and good nesting conditions. In other words, they want to live inside your house. They enter through the smallest imaginable holes and cracks. Young ones can worm their way through a 1/4-in. opening. Take a very close look around the outside of your house, and then caulk, plug or do whatever it takes to close every entry point you can find. Worn weather stripping under doors can be a perfect, easy entry point for mice looking for a warm place to winter. Replacing it is usually as simple as taking the door off the hinges and slipping a new weather strip into the slots. Take the old weather stripping to the home center to find a match.

Prune for healthier bushes

PROFESSIONAL
COST: $40 per hour

YOUR COST: $0

SAVINGS: $40

COMPLEXITY
Simple

TOOLS
Pruner

Too often, trees and bushes become eyesores because they're ragged and scraggly, misshapen, too big and full of ugly dead wood. And then, you're left with the difficult chore of digging them out and planting expensive new ones. But a half hour of pruning once or twice a year will prevent this problem. A simple trim will make your bushes and small trees more attractive, encourage better flowering and growth, and maintain their ideal size. The following tips will guide you through the basics.

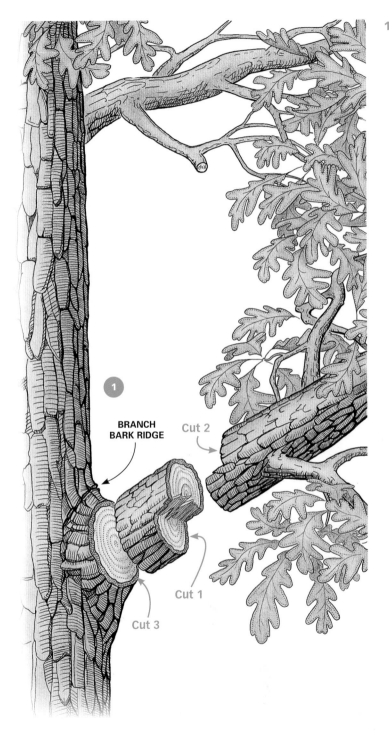

BRANCH BARK RIDGE

Cut 2

Cut 1

Cut 3

1. **Trouble-free tree pruning.** Prune midsize branches without damaging the tree by cutting them in three stages. Make the first cut (1) on the underside about 8 in. from the trunk, cutting a third of the way up. Make the next cut (2) at the top of the branch 3 in. past the first cut. Finally, cut the remaining stump off at the trunk, just past the slightly raised area, called the branch bark ridge, making the cut perpendicular to the branch to minimize the exposed surface.

pro tips!

➤ You can prune almost everything in early spring. Just be sure to get to it!

2. **Cut out dead, damaged, diseased and deranged branches.** Some arborists call these the "4 Ds." Start with the dead and damaged branches, because they make the plant look bad, and encourage rot and disease. Also cut out wilted, dried or diseased branches as soon as you spot them, to remove the disease before it spreads. "Deranged" includes a broad range of branches that cross and loop down to the ground or simply look out of character with the bush (stick out at an odd angle or grow alongside the trunk). This pruning also thins out the bush, opening its interior to more light and air, which encourages fuller, healthier growth.

3. **Prune out about one-third of the branches of bushes that grow from canes.** Cane-type bushes, such as forsythia and hydrangea, usually send up new canes from their roots every year. In general, prune out the oldest (larger) wood to control the bush height. It's also OK to trim out newer canes to thin the interior of the plant and let in light as well as to control its spread. If one of these bushes has gotten too big and out of control, you can often cut off all the canes and the roots will send up new shoots. You'll have a nice new bush in a year or two. Note: All bush categories have exceptions to these rules. So know your plants!

CROSSING BRANCH

LARGE OLDER CANE

First year · **Second year** · SIDE BRANCHES · BRANCH TIP

HEDGE SHEARS

DON'T

4. **Clip off branch tips to promote small-branch growth and denser foliage.** This "heading off" technique channels more growth energy to smaller side branches, which will then fill in vacant areas. Make this cut at a side branch or 1/4 in. beyond a bud (first year). Be selective and watch the results from the previous year to help gauge future growth. It works best on bushes and trees that grow mostly from one or a few stalks, as opposed to bushes that continually send up new shoots (suckers), like lilacs and forsythia.

5. **Don't trim new growth with hedge shears!** It's tempting to grab the hedge shears and shape a bush by cutting off the branch tips. This "flattop haircut" approach may look fine for a year or two, but it stimulates growth on the outermost branches, forces the bush to grow into an unnatural shape (your idea rather than the plant's) and fails to control size. The bush actually grows larger and becomes more difficult to bring back to size without being ruined. The exception is hedge-type bushes.

6. **Remove entire branches to shape the bush and control its size.** If neglected, many bushes get too big and dense. While the foliage might look OK this year, next year it just might be too big to prune back without butchering it. Instead, it's better to control size and shape by selectively pruning out a few entire branches each year. Cut them at a larger branch or the trunk. This also opens the plant to light and encourages healthy growth from the interior.

7. **Prune evergreens lightly.** Unlike cane-type bushes, evergreens and other "nonsucker-type" bushes grow from their existing stems. They develop a more permanent branch framework and usually need less pruning. If your landscaping was well planned, these bushes, especially evergreens, will grow to fit their spot with relatively little help. They'll need only a light annual pruning to remove dead branches and to control size and shape.

8. **Make pruning cuts just beyond the branch "collar."** The branch collar is the bark swell that encircles the branch. If left intact, this collar will soon grow over and cover the wound. Don't leave stubs. They'll rot and might become diseased.

9. **Don't force a big bush to conform to a small space by pruning.** It can be done, but it's easier to pull out an overgrown bush and plant one that will mature at a size that better fits the space.

Replace a toilet seat

PROFESSIONAL
COST: $80

YOUR COST: $30

SAVINGS: $50

COMPLEXITY
Simple

TOOLS
Deep-well socket

Socket wrench

Screwdriver

MATERIALS
Toilet seat

Installing a new toilet seat is an easy two-minute job: Just set the seat in place and tighten the nuts. Removing the old seat, on the other hand, can be a frustrating ordeal. Often, the bolts that fasten the seat are so corroded that you simply can't unscrew the nuts. First, take a look at the bolts that secure the seat. If the bolts or nuts are plastic, they can't corrode and will come off easily. Simply pry open the cover behind the seat to expose the bolt's head. Unscrew the bolt with pliers or a screwdriver while you hold the nut underneath with pliers.

DEEP-WELL SOCKET

1. If the bolts are metal, you might be able to unscrew the nuts with pliers, but the best tool for this job is a socket wrench equipped with a deep-well socket. Most toilet seats require a 1/2-in. socket. The deep socket fits over the long bolt and grips the nut tightly. Most metal bolts aren't covered by a flip-open cover; all you have to do is turn the nut counter-clockwise. Go ahead and twist as hard as you can. If the bolt is brass or badly cor-roded steel, you might break it off, which is just fine. If the nut won't budge, douse it with a penetrating spray lubricant such as WD-40. Hold a rag behind the nut to catch the overspray. Give the lubricant 15 minutes to penetrate, then try again. If the bolt spins as you turn the nut and doesn't loosen, or the bolt just spins, try this:

2. If lubricant won't free the nut, grab your drill, drill bit collection and safety glasses. Using a 1/16-in. bit, drill into the bolt where it meets the nut. Drill 1/4 in. into the bolt. Next, enlarge the hole with a 1/8-in. bit, followed by a 3/16-in. bit. Then try the socket wrench again. Your goal now isn't to unscrew the nut but to break off the bolt as you turn the nut. If the bolt won't break, keep enlarging the hole. Eventually you'll weaken the bolt enough to break it. Remove the bolts and now you can remove the old seat and install the new one.

pro tips!

➤ Before you go to buy a replacement toilet seat, take measurements of the old one and/or take a picture to use as a reference. Toilet seats come in many different sizes and shapes and you don't want to get one home and have to return it because it doesn't fit.

Remove ceiling texture

PROFESSIONAL
COST: $1,000

YOUR COST: $100

SAVINGS: $900

COMPLEXITY
Moderate

TOOLS
6-in. putty knife

12-in. drywall taping
  knife

Pump sprayer

Mud pan

Ladder

MATERIALS
Painter's tape

Plastic dropcloths

Popcorn ceilings were all the rage back in the 1960s and '70s. Applying the texture to drywall and plaster ceilings was a quick and easy way to hide imperfections and didn't require any painting afterward. But the rough texture catches lots of dust and cobwebs, and it can be a real pain to match if you have cracks or holes in need of patching. Removing popcorn texture from a ceiling is a messy chore but worth the effort if the ceiling underneath is in good shape. Here are some tips to take some of the pain out of scraping the popcorn texture off your ceiling.

1. **Do a scrape test.** Before you go to all the trouble of prepping the room, try scraping a small area. Try it dry first, then dampen the texture with water and try again. Some texture comes off easily without water, but in most cases wetting is best. If the water doesn't soak in and soften the texture, the ceiling has probably been painted or paint was added to the texture mix. In that case, wetting the ceiling may not help, and you'll have to decide whether you want to tackle a really tough scraping job or choose another way to hide your popcorn ceiling.

2. **Prep for a big mess.** Cover floors and walls with plastic dropcloths. Don't use canvas dropcloths because water can soak through. Cleanup is easier with plastic too, because you can just ball it all up when you're done working and throw it in the trash. Leave the plastic in place after scraping to catch the mess you'll make repairing and sanding the ceiling later.

CAUTION

Any popcorn ceiling installed before 1980 might contain asbestos—a known cause of lung cancer. Before trying to scrape off any popcorn texture, contact your local health department and ask about getting a sample tested. If the test comes back positive, cover the popcorn with new drywall or tongue-and-groove planks, or hire an asbestos abatement contractor to remove the popcorn.

3. **Get the furniture out.** If possible, remove all furniture from the room you'll be working in. Scraping popcorn is messy work, and you won't want furniture in your way every time you move the ladder around. If moving everything out of the room isn't possible, cluster it and cover it with dropcloths.

4. **Remove ceiling fixtures and fans.** You might think it's easier to leave light fixtures and ceiling fans in place, but they'll just be in your way and get covered with wet popcorn. Plus, you don't want to accidentally spray water into an electrical fixture.

5. **Protect can lights from water spray.** If you have recessed "can" lights, stuff newspaper or rosin paper inside them to keep them dry. Also, make sure the power to those fixtures is turned off at the electrical panel.

6. **Cover electrical boxes.** Shut off the power to any electrical junction boxes in the ceiling and cover them with painter's tape to keep the wiring dry when spraying water on the popcorn. Overlap the sides of the junction box with the tape, and then trim around the perimeter with a utility knife, being careful not to nick the wires.

JUNCTION BOX

7. **Wet it with a pump sprayer.** For easier scraping and practically no dust, use a garden pump sprayer to mist the ceiling and let it soak in for about 15 minutes before scraping. Only give it a light misting—too much water could damage the drywall or loosen the joint tape. If the texture hasn't softened after 15 minutes or so, spray it again and wait another 10 to 15 minutes. If the texture still hasn't softened, it might be painted, or paint might have been mixed into the texture before application. In either case, water won't easily penetrate. If the texture is painted, you might be able to dry-scrape it first to expose some of the unpainted texture and follow up with wet scraping. If the texture has paint mixed in, you might have to dry-scrape the whole ceiling or cover it up with drywall or tongue-and-groove (shiplap) boards.

8. **Get two scrapers.** A stiff 6-in. putty knife works great for smaller areas, and a 12-in. drywall taping knife helps you get a wide area done faster.

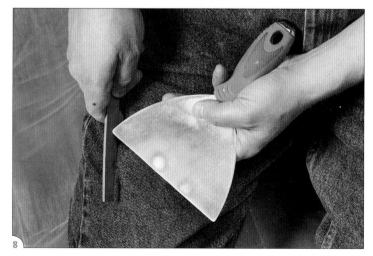

9. **Work in small sections.** Only spray and scrape a small area at a time—about 4 x 4 ft. If you work too large of an area at once, the popcorn might dry before you have time to scrape it off. If that happens, respray the area and wait another 10 to 15 minutes before scraping.

10. **Tame the mess with a mud pan.** Use a mud pan—the kind for holding drywall joint compound—to catch the wet popcorn before it hits the floor. That way, you're not tracking it all over the place when you walk and move the ladder around. Also, use the edge of the pan to clean off your scraper when it gets loaded up with wet popcorn.

11. **After scraping...** Scraping alone won't leave you with a paint-ready ceiling. You'll probably have small dings and gouges to fix. At a minimum, you'll have to sand the ceiling to get it perfectly smooth before painting.

PROFESSIONAL
COST: $1,000

YOUR COST: $50

SAVINGS: $950

COMPLEXITY
Simple

TOOLS
Moving and lifting
straps

Moving blankets

MATERIALS
Mover's stretch
plastic film

Move furniture

Whether you're rearranging furniture in your living room or relocating, moving furniture is a big job. We'll show you some simple techniques for moving heavy, awkward items without wrecking your back, your house or the furniture.

1. **Plan where it lands.** If you're moving, decide beforehand which furniture will go where. Before you move, sketch a floor plan with the correct measurements of each room, measure your furniture and create your layout. Then, as you move things in, you (or your helpers, if you're not there) can place your furniture in the correct spot and not have to touch it again. To make it easier on everyone, tape a copy of the plan to the wall of each room so people can tell at a glance where things go.

2. **Carry tall items high and low.** A tall dresser, filing cabinet or shelving unit is awkward to handle. Make it a two-person job. Tip the item backward at an angle and have one person carry the top while the other carries the bottom. This centers the weight and keeps the item from swinging out of control. Transporting the item up or down stairs is easier too, since the carrying angle will roughly match the slope of the stairs.

3. **"Hook" chairs around corners**. A large easy chair can be the opposite of easy to move. Follow the example of pro movers and "hook" large chairs around corners. Turn the chair on its side so it looks like an "L" and move it back-first through the doorway. Then curl it (hook it) around the door frame and slip it through.

4. **Stand couches on end**. If you ever have to maneuver a couch down a hallway and through a door, you may find it almost impossible to carry it horizontally and make the turn into the room. Before you enter the hallway, place the couch on its end and slide it to the doorway. You'll almost always be able to hook it (see Tip 3) through the door. If it's a bit taller than the door opening, start the top away from the door and gain several inches of clearance.

SHOULDER DOLLY

5

6

5. Pick up some straps. Moving and lifting straps take the weight off your back by relying on leverage and large muscle groups. They also leave your hands free to maneuver awkward items. However, they can be tricky to use on stairs because the weight shifts completely to the downhill mover. Look for lifting straps that can be adjusted for different-length objects as well as for different-size movers.

6. Don't carry or drag —slide. You can buy furniture slides in many shapes and sizes at home centers and online. It's also easy to make your own sliders from plastic container covers, Frisbees, bedspreads, moving blankets, towels and carpet remnants. Use hard plastic sliders for carpeting, and soft, padded sliders for hard flooring.

7. Protect furniture with blankets and plastic. Moving blankets are invaluable for protecting the items you're moving as well as your house. Sure, renting them is cheap, but you can buy several for just a few dollars more at home centers or uhaul.com and always have them on hand. (You'll use them for all kinds of other things too.) To prevent damaging the finish and fragile edges of dressers, tables and other furniture, wrap the items completely with moving blankets and secure the blanket with stretch film. You can get a 20-in. x 1,500-ft. roll of stretch film at home centers and moving outfitters.

8. Make a mattress sling. Trying to wrestle a heavy, floppy mattress anywhere is tough. Many mattresses have handles, but they're not intended for carrying. They're actually made to help you position the mattress, so they're not very strong. Here's an easier way to carry a mattress: Make a simple rope sling that will give you and your helper a lot more control. Thread the rope through the mattress handles and attach your grips as shown. Flip the mattress over so the sling is on the bottom and you're on your way.

Slip a 5-in. piece of 1-in. PVC pipe over the rope ends and then loop and tie each end to create a comfortable sling grip.

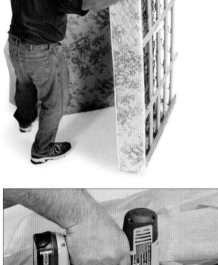

9. **Cut and fold a box spring.** Is your box spring too big to fit in your stairway or around a tight corner? You could buy a "split" box spring designed specifically for this (and pay several hundred bucks) or cut your existing box spring and fold it so it fits. Sound extreme? There's actually a simple, ingenious way to cut and fold your box spring without wrecking it.

> **Cut the frame.** Remove the fabric covering (the most tedious part of this whole process is removing the staples) and place the box spring face down. Pull back the mattress cover along each side and cut through the frame just to the left or right of the middle crosspiece (don't cut through the crosspiece itself). Do this on both sides and in the center.

> **Fold it.** You can now fold the box spring like a book, as shown, and move it. Secure it with a strap to prevent it from springing open.

> **Put it back together.** Screw a 1x2 along the center crosspiece cuts and against the inside of the outer frame to reinforce them. Then staple the fabric covering in place.

Chapter 7

DIY Projects Beginners Can Build

Multipurpose shelves

Store-bought shelving units are either hard to assemble, flimsy or awfully expensive. Here's a better solution. These shelves are strong, easy to build and budget-friendly. The sturdy shelf unit shown at left is sized to hold standard records and storage boxes. If you want deeper storage, build the shelves 24 in. deep and buy 24-in.-deep boxes. If you prefer to use plastic storage bins, measure the size of the containers and modify the shelf and upright spacing to fit.

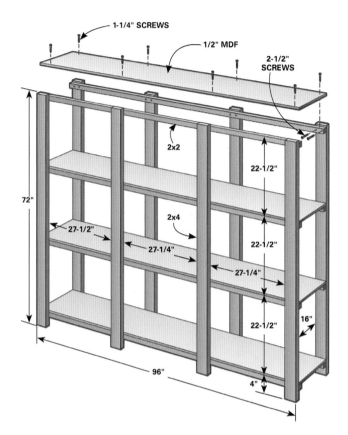

1-1/4" SCREWS

1/2" MDF

2-1/2" SCREWS

2x2

72"

22-1/2"

27-1/2"

2x4

27-1/4"

22-1/2"

27-1/4"

22-1/2"

16"

96"

4"

Refer to the dimensions in the illustration to mark the location of the horizontal 2x2 on the back of four 2x4s. Also mark the position of the 2x4 uprights on the 2x2s. Then simply line up the marks and screw the 2x2s to the 2x4s with pairs of 2-1/2-in. wood screws. Be sure to keep the 2x2s and 2x4s at right angles. Cut a 4 x 8-ft. sheet of 1/2-in. MDF, plywood or OSB into 16-in.-wide strips and screw it to the 2x2s to connect the two frames and form the shelving unit.

Customizing your shelves

You can modify the sturdy storage shelves above and create a great-looking storage center like this one and the one on p. 202. Simply add one shelf and change the 22-1/2-in. measurement to 14 in. and the 4-in. measurement to 6 in. Apply the finish of your choice.

Super-simple workbench

This sturdy 30-in. x 6-ft.-long workbench is the ultimate in simplicity. It's made from only fifteen 8-ft.-long 2x4s and one sheet of 1/2-in. plywood. Follow the cutting diagrams to cut the parts: Figure B to cut the plywood tops, then Figure C to cut all the framing. Use the lengths provided in the Cutting List. You can either screw the framing together with 3-in. screws or hand- or power-nail it together with 3-in. nails. Screw the plywood down with 1-5/8-in. screws. To make these project plans even easier to follow, we tinted the parts that get added at each step.

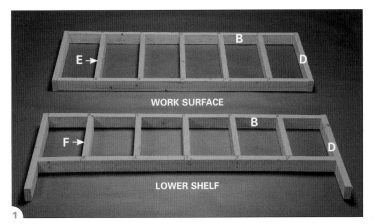

Figure A
Main workbench parts

1. Assemble the frames for the work surface and lower shelf.

Accessorize it!

➤ **Lighting.** Good light is mandatory for any workbench. Buy a 4-ft. shop light and screw it right to the underside of the top shelf.

➤ **Power strip.** Forget extension cords. Mount a power strip to one of the legs and you'll have all the power you need for tools and chargers. Use its switch to control the light.

➤ **Pegboard.** Whether you cover the whole back or just the lower half, keep down the bench clutter by stowing all of those tools you use every day within easy reach.

➤ **Bench vise.** Yes, it'll cost as much as or more than the bench, but what workbench would be complete without one?

2. Screw the legs to the work surface frame.

3. Flip over the bench and attach the lower shelf frame.

4. Screw the plywood to the frames.

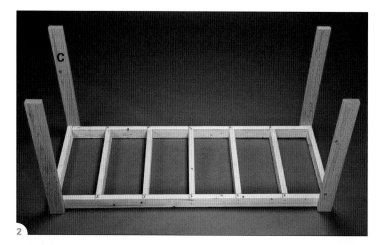

pro tips!

➤ Use paint cans to support the lower shelf frame when you're attaching it to the main workbench legs.

Figure B
Plywood cutting diagram

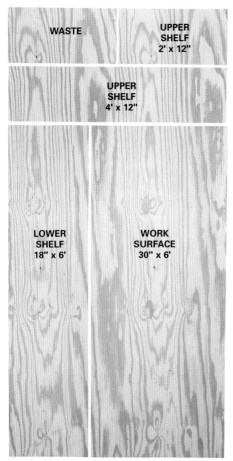

Figure C
2x4 usage diagram

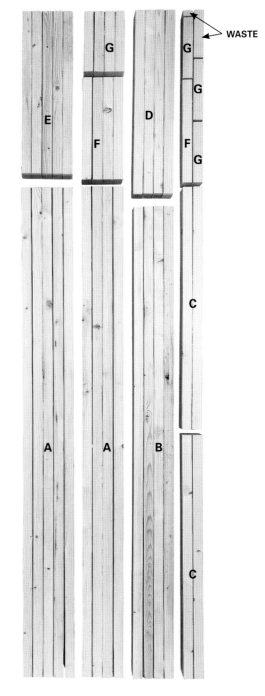

Cutting List

KEY	QTY.	SIZE & DESCRIPTION
A	9	71-7/8" (backer boards, upper shelf legs and rims)
B	4	68-7/8" (work surface and lower shelf rim)
C	4	35-1/2" (legs)
D	4	27" (end rims)
E	5	24" (work surface joists)
F	5	15" (lower shelf joists)
G	7	9" (upper shelf joists)

5. Assemble the top shelf frame.

6. Add the plywood.

7. Attach the top shelf legs upside down.

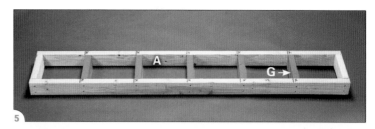

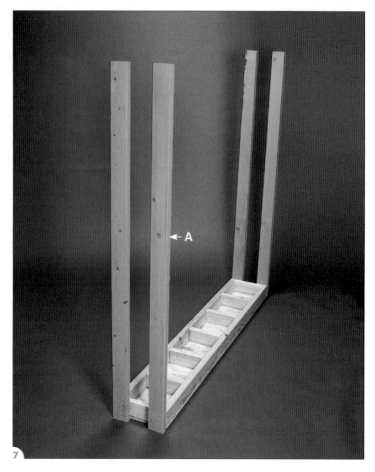

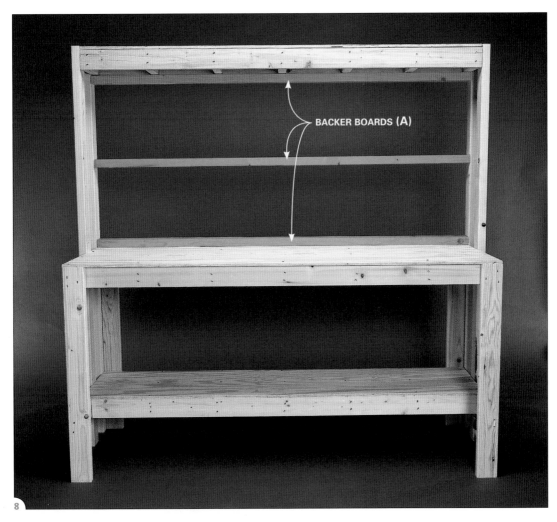

8. Screw the legs to the bench and add the backer boards.

Easy outdoor bench

If you're looking for a simple bench, take a look at this one built by Aldo Leopold, whom many consider the father of wildlife ecology and if this bench was good enough for him, it's definitely good enough for the rest of us! A little research led to this sturdy design, which can be built quickly with a few 2x8s, glue and screws. Best of all, it's amazingly comfortable, perfect for bird-watching—even for two people.

1. Mark one end of the 2x8 x 10-ft. board at a 22-1/2-degree angle with a Speed square or protractor, then cut with a circular saw. Make a mark 36 in. away and repeat the cut at the same angle. Cut the remaining front leg and two back legs from the same piece. Cut the seat and the backrest from the 2x8 x 8-ft. board.

2. Fasten the legs together. Stack and clamp the seat and backrest to the edge of the worktable as guides, and then align the legs against them. Spread adhesive on the front leg, set the rear leg in place, and fasten the legs together with three 2-1/2-in. screws.

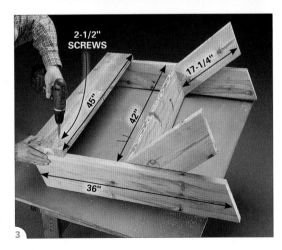

3. Attach the seat and backrest. Stand the two ends up, 42 in. apart, spread glue on the tops of the rear legs, and screw the seat in place. Lay the bench on the worktable and attach the backrest with glue and screws.

pro tips!

To make a simple project even simpler, remember these tips:
➤ Be sure to assemble the legs (Step 2) so they're mirror images of each other, and not facing the same direction.
➤ Use clamps or a helper to hold the legs upright when securing the seat.
➤ Predrill all your screw holes to prevent splitting the wood.

Materials List

ITEM	QTY.
2x8 x 8' cedar, redwood or treated lumber (seat and backrest)	1
2x8 x 10' cedar, redwood or treated lumber (front and read legs)	1
Exterior construction adhesive	
2-1/2" galvanized deck screws	

Behind-the-door shelves

The space behind a door is a storage spot that's often overlooked. One way to utilize it is to build a set of shallow shelves and mount it to the wall. Measure the distance between the door hinge and the wall and subtract an inch. This is the maximum depth of the shelves. Use 1x4s for the sides, top and shelves. Screw the sides to the top. Then screw three 1x2 hanging strips to the sides: one top and bottom and one centered. Nail metal shelf standards to the sides. Complete the shelves by nailing a 1x2 trim piece to the sides and top. The 1x2 dresses up the shelf unit and keeps the shelves from falling off the shelf clips.

Locate the studs. Drill clearance holes and screw the shelves to the studs with 2-1/2-in. wood screws. Put a rubber bumper on the frame to protect the door.

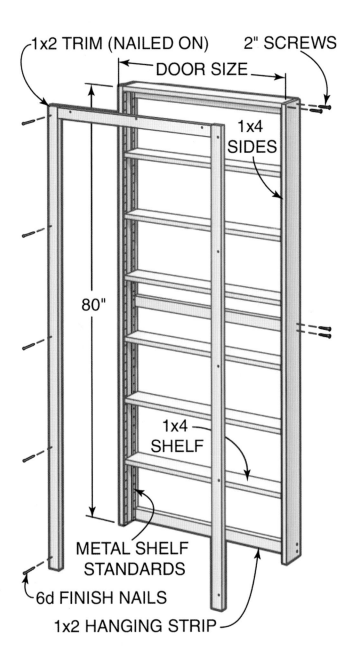

1x2 TRIM (NAILED ON)   2" SCREWS

DOOR SIZE

1x4 SIDES

80"

1x4 SHELF

METAL SHELF STANDARDS

6d FINISH NAILS

1x2 HANGING STRIP

Figure A
Behind-the-door shelves

Knock-apart table

This table is made from a full sheet of 5/8-in. plywood for the interlocking base stand and a sheet of 3/4-in. plywood for the work surface and shelves. You'll also need four 10-ft. lengths of 1x3 pine for the edge banding and cleats. Cut two 30-in.-high by 48-in.-long pieces from the 5/8-in. plywood for the base pieces. Then cut a slightly oversize 5/8-in.-wide slot in the bottom half of one base and in the top half of the other. Make both slots about 15-1/2 in. long. Assemble the base and position the top so the corners are aligned with the legs. Screw loose-fitting 12-in.-long 1x3s along each side of each leg to hold everything stable.

The table is much more stable if you use the 3/4-in. waste from the top to make triangular braces (which also act as shelves) with 20-in.-long sides. Using 1-1/4-in. drywall screws, attach 1x2s to the base about 12 in. up from the floor and screw the shelves down.

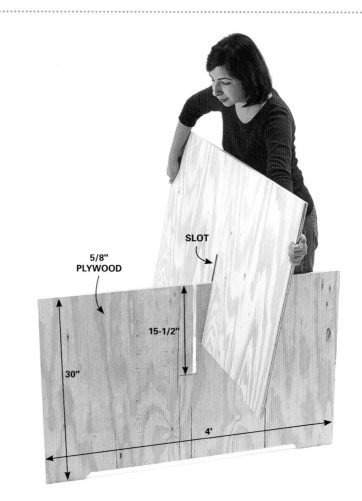

5/8" PLYWOOD

SLOT

15-1/2"

30"

4'

LOOSE
FIT
AGAINST
LEG

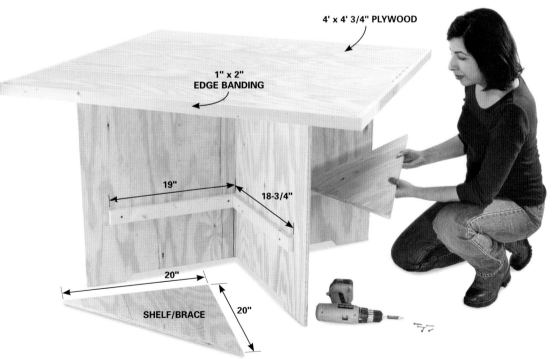

4' x 4' 3/4" PLYWOOD

1" x 2"
EDGE BANDING

19"

18-3/4"

20"

20"

SHELF/BRACE

Light-duty table

If you ever need a light-duty work surface anywhere in the house for sewing, painting or school projects, this one's for you. Get to the home center and buy an inexpensive hollow-core door; four toilet flanges; a 10-ft. length of 3-in. PVC pipe; 16 No. 10, 1-1/4-in.-long screws and a tube of construction adhesive. Inside of a half hour, you'll have the flanges glued and screwed to the door and be ready to slip in the 30-in.-long PVC legs.

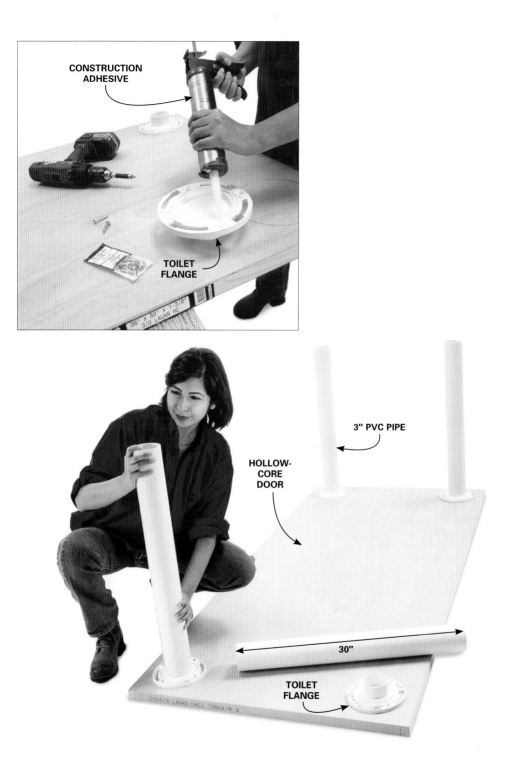

CONSTRUCTION
ADHESIVE

TOILET
FLANGE

3" PVC PIPE

HOLLOW-
CORE
DOOR

30"

TOILET
FLANGE

Chapter 8

DIY Skills You Can Master

A smooth, fast polyurethane finish

You may think a brush is the best tool for applying polyurethane finish, but think again! Use this method for a perfect finish every time.

Lose the dust. Wipe down every square inch of the workpiece with a lint-free cotton cloth dampened with mineral spirits or denatured alcohol.

6" MICROFIBER ROLLER

VARNISH IN BAKING SHEET

Roll on poly fast—then quit. Dampen the roller with mineral spirits and roll the poly on all of the large flat areas and cabinet interiors. Coat the surface and quit. Don't continue to work the finish.

A clean work area is key

The more dust free the project and the surrounding surfaces, the less work you'll have and the more flawless your finish will be. Before you start, vacuum the project, the workbench and the floor. Under the piece to be finished, spread out 6-mil poly to protect the floor from drips and spills and to make cleanup easy. Reuse these sheets several times, then toss them. Don't finish on the same day you sand; the dust stays in the air for hours. Start finishing with clean clothes and hair.

1. **Wipe down with mineral spirits.** Wipe down the project with a tack cloth, or a lint-free cloth saturated with solvent. You can use an old, clean cotton T-shirt for this and the wipe-on step shown later. This step removes nearly all traces of dust. It only takes a few minutes for the solvent to evaporate so you can get started on finishing. Don't use water; it'll raise the grain and you'll have to sand again.

2. **Use a roller on large flat surfaces.** You can get the poly on fast and evenly with little rollers—no brushstrokes, puddles or

thin spots. Some rollers may cause bubbles, but 6-in. microfiber rollers dampened with mineral spirits work great. There's always a bit of leftover lint, but only on the first coat. A Teflon baking tray makes a great rolling pan.

3. **Check for imprefections.** Don't worry when you see the finish right after you lay it down. It'll look like it's full of flaws. Just roll it out and use the raking light to make sure the surface is completely covered. Don't keep working the finish. Let it be, and it will flatten out. Keep a can of spray poly handy in case of bubbles. A light mist knocks them out. After each coat, redip the roller in mineral spirits and put it into a zippered plastic bag for the next coat and leave the wet tray to dry. In a couple of hours, the dried poly just peels right out of the pan. It's usually best to put two coats on cabinet interiors and sides, and three coats on tabletops for extra protection.

4. **Finish both sides at once.** With a solid wood top like this one,

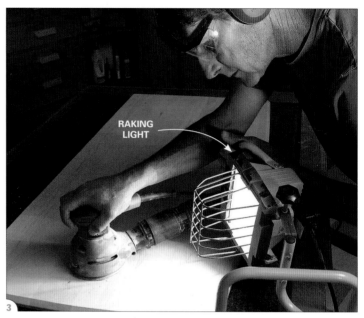

Use a light held at a low, raking angle to check for scratches, dirt and any other imperfections while you sand and apply finish coats.

Finish both sides at once. Coat the bottom first and then flip over the top, resting it on standoffs while you roll the finish on the top. the painter's pyramid (standoff) shown is available at home centers.

Use wipe-on poly for small or tight areas. Dribble wipe-on poly on the rag and wet the entire area. Sand between coats with extra-fine sanding pads.

pro tips!

➤ **Sand out the pencil marks.** Begin by drawing light, squiggly pencil lines on the surface at each grit stage. When the pencil lines disappear, you're ready to move on to the next grit. You're wasting your time sanding coarse, open-grained woods like ash or oak super smooth. Start at 80 grit and end with 100 or 120 grit. Sanding through all the grits to 220 grit won't improve the finish one bit. But with closed-grained woods like maple or birch, don't skip any grit steps, and go all the way to 220 grit.

finish both the top and the bottom surfaces, even if the bottom won't show. Skip this step and the top can twist, cup or warp. To save drying time, coat the bottom and then immediately flip it over to finish the top. Right after the top is rolled out, roll the edges and then go around them with a dry foam brush to eliminate any drips or thick spots. You can skip the final coat on the underside. Being short a single coat on the underside isn't a big deal.

5. **Zero cleanup with wipe-on poly.** After the roll-on coats are dry, use wipe-on oil poly (use the same sheen you chose for the roll-on poly) for the face frames, legs, doors or any other narrow, small or intricate areas. Do this after the large areas are dry so you don't smudge adjacent areas. This is a great method because only two things get dirty: a glove and a cotton rag, both of which you can toss after each coat. (Spread them out to dry first.) You can

put on two to four coats in one day depending on the temperature and humidity. There are no drips, sags or runs—ever. And because it dries so fast, there's rarely a dust problem. The downside? Because the coats are so thin, you need lots of them. You can put on as many as eight coats of wipe-on when two rolled coats would do the trick.

6. **Sand with pads and paper.** Lightly sand between coats with extra-fine synthetic sanding pads. The goal is to roughen the surface a bit and rub out dust motes, hairs and drips. If there are stubborn nibs that stand up to the pads, grab 280-grit and be more aggressive. Then just wipe off the dust with mineral spirits and apply another coat.

7. **The final coat gets special treatment.** For the final coat, vacuum the work area again and let the dust settle overnight. After the finish is on, let the project dry and you're done!

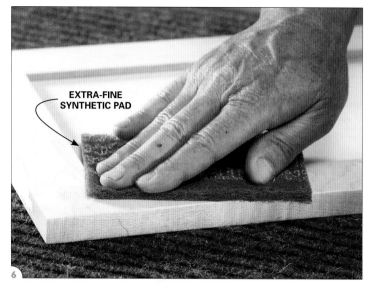

EXTRA-FINE SYNTHETIC PAD

Lightly sand between coats. Wipe off dust whiskers with extra-fine sanding pads. For larger blemishes, use 280-grit paper. The raking light will show you when the surface is smooth.

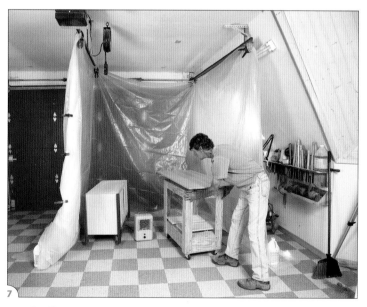

Let the final coat dry in a dust-free area. For big projects, build yourself a temporary drying booth with poly sheeting. If it's cool, use an electric space heater to hasten drying and shorten the time that dust can become embedded in the finish.

pro tips!

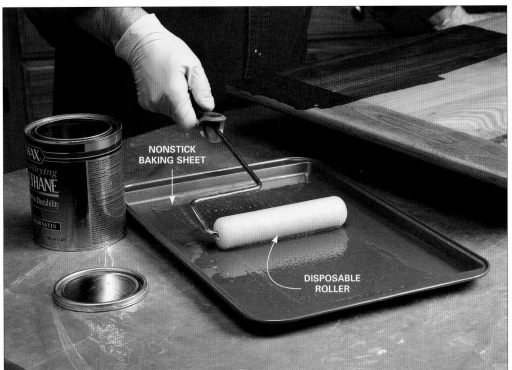

NONSTICK BAKING SHEET

DISPOSABLE ROLLER

Zero cleanup

Forget brushes when it comes to varnishing a ton of trim or big, flat areas like cabinets. Use a 4-in. disposable roller and a nonstick, lipped baking sheet. Pour some varnish into the tray and use it just like a paint rolling tray. Keep adding varnish as you need it, but try to plan so you end up with an empty tray. When you're through, toss the roller sleeve and let the wet varnish dry in the pan. When it dries, just peel the varnish film right out of the pan.

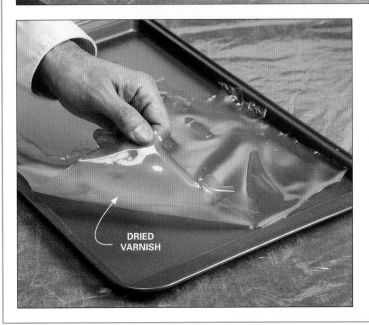

DRIED VARNISH

Refinish furniture without stripping

Stripping furniture is a messy, time-consuming process. And sometimes the results aren't as great as you had hoped. Fortunately, you don't always have to resort to stripping to restore your furniture to its original luster. For an easier alternative, we enlisted a professional furniture restoration specialist. We'll show you his tips for cleaning, repairing and restoring finishes without all the messy chemical strippers and tedious sanding. You'll save tons of time.

CAUTION

If you think your piece of furniture is a valuable antique, consult an expert before you do anything.

1. **Assess the finish with mineral spirits.**
   Before you start any repairs or touch-up, wipe on mineral spirits to help you decide what your next steps should be. The mineral spirits temporarily saturates the finish to reveal how the piece of furniture will look with nothing more than a coat of wipe-on clear finish. Don't worry; this won't harm the finish. If it looks good, all you have to do is clean the surface and apply an oil-based wipe-on finish. If the surface looks bad even when wetted with mineral spirits, you'll have to take other measures to restore the finish. We show some of these in the following steps.

2. **Clean it up.** A thorough cleaning is an important first step in any furniture renewal project. Removing decades of dirt and grime often restores much of the original luster. It may be hard to believe, but it's perfectly OK to wash furniture with soap and water.

   Use liquid Ivory dish soap mixed with water. Mix in the same proportion you would to wash dishes. Dip a sponge into the solution, wring it out and use it to gently scrub the surface. A paintbrush works great for cleaning carvings and moldings. When you're done scrubbing with the soapy water, rinse the surface with a wrung-out sponge and clear water. Then dry it with a clean towel.

3. **Scrape paint without damaging the finish.** Paint spatters are common on old furniture, and most of the time you can remove them easily without damaging the finish. Here's a pro trick to turn an ordinary straightedge razor into a delicate paint scraper. First, wrap a layer of masking tape around each end of the blade, and then bend the blade slightly so it's curved.

   The masking tape holds the blade slightly off the surface so you can knock off paint spatters without the blade even touching the wood. Hold the blade perpendicular to the surface. The tape also keeps you from accidentally gouging the wood with the sharp corner of the blade. The curved blade allows you to adjust the depth of the scraper. If you tilt the blade a little, the curved center section will come closer to the surface to allow for removing really thin layers of paint.

2

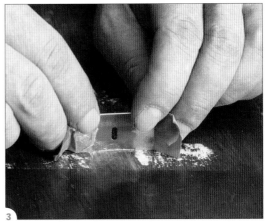

3

4. Replace missing wood with epoxy.
If you discover missing veneer, chipped wood or a damaged molding, you can fix it easily with epoxy putty.

When it's hardened, the epoxy is light colored and about the density of wood. You can shape, sand and stain it like wood too, so it blends right in. Quickwood and KwikWood are two brands of this epoxy. You'll find it at home centers and specialty wood-working stores.

To use this type of epoxy, you slice off a piece with a razor blade or utility knife and knead it in your gloved hand. When the two parts are completely blended to a consistent color and the epoxy putty starts to get sticky, it's ready to use. You'll have about five or 10 minutes to apply the epoxy to the repair before it starts to harden. That's why you should only slice off as much as you can use quickly.

Photo A shows how to replace missing veneer. Here are a few things you can do before the putty starts to harden to reduce the amount of sanding and shaping later. First, smooth and shape the epoxy with your finger (Photo B). Wet it with water first to prevent the epoxy from sticking. Then use the edge of a straightedge razor to scrape the surface almost level with the surrounding veneer. If you're repairing wood with an open grain,

A

Fill the damage with epoxy. When the epoxy putty is thoroughly mixed, press it into the area to be repaired.

B

Smooth the putty. Use your wetted finger to smooth the putty. Press the putty until it's level with the surrounding veneer.

like oak, add grain details by making little slices with a razor while the epoxy is soft (Photo C).

After the epoxy hardens completely, which usually takes a few hours, you

Add wood grain. On open-grain wood like this oak, use a razor blade to add grain marks.

also use spray adhesive or even plain wood glue to attach the sandpaper.

Blend the repair into the surrounding veneer by painting on gel stain to match the color and pattern of the existing grain. You could use stain touch-up markers, but our pro prefers gel stain because it's thick enough to act like paint and can be wiped off with a rag dampened in mineral spirits if you goof up or want to start over.

Choose two colors of stain that match the light and dark areas of the wood. Put a dab of both on a scrap of wood and create a range of colors by blending a bit of the two. Now you can use an artist's brush to create the grain (Photo E). If the sheen of the patch doesn't match the rest of the wood when the stain dries, you can recoat the entire surface with wipe-on finish to even it out.

can sand and stain the repair. You can stick self-adhesive sandpaper to tongue depressors or craft sticks to make precision sanding blocks (Photo D). You can

Sand the epoxy. Sand carefully to avoid removing the surrounding finish. Make a detail sander by gluing sandpaper to a thin strip of wood.

Stain the epoxy to match. Stain the patch with gel stain to match the color and pattern of the grain. Match the stain color to the light and dark areas of the wood.

5. **Get rid of dents.** You can often get rid of small dents by wetting them. The moisture swells the crushed wood fibers back to their original shape. (You can't fix cuts or gouges this way, though.) Moisture must penetrate the wood for this to work. Finishes prevent water from penetrating, so our pro suggests making a bunch of tiny slits with a razor blade to allow the water to penetrate. Use the corner of the blade and keep the blade parallel to the grain direction. Next, fill the dent with water and wait until it dries. If the dent is less deep but still visible, you can repeat the process. As with most of the repairs we talk about here, the repaired surface may need a coat of wipe-on finish to look its best.

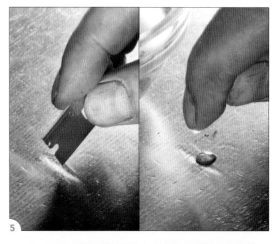

6. **Restore the color with gel stain.** It's amazing what a coat of gel stain can do to restore a tired-looking piece of furniture. The cool part is that you don't need to strip the old finish for this to work. We demonstrated the tip on this round oak table.

   The finish was worn and faded, so we loaded a soft cloth with dark gel stain and worked it into the surface. Then we wiped it off with a clean cloth. It was a surprising transformation. Of course, gel stain won't eliminate dark water stains or cover bad defects, but it will hide fine scratches and color in areas where the finish has worn away.

   There are other products, but our pro prefers gel stain because he finds it easier to control the color and leave a thicker coat if necessary. Also, since it doesn't soak in quite as readily as thinner stains, gel stain is somewhat reversible. Before it dries, you can remove it with mineral spirits if you don't

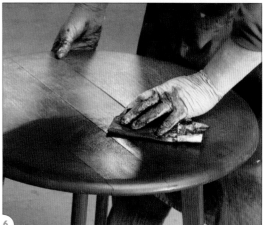

like the results. Gel stains offer some protection, but for a more durable finish or to even out the sheen, let the stain dry overnight and then apply a coat of wipe-on finish.

7. **Fix white rings.** White rings can be easy to get rid of, or they can be a real nightmare. First, slather the ring with petroleum jelly and let it sit overnight. The oil from the petroleum jelly will often penetrate the finish and remove the ring or at least make it less visible.

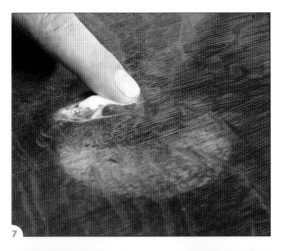

7

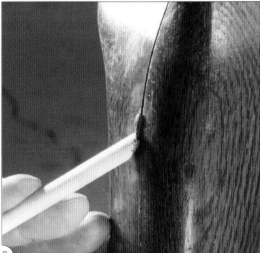

8

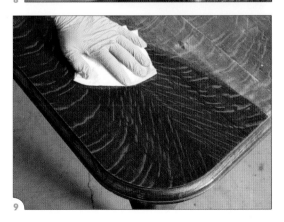

9

If that doesn't work, you can try a product such as Homax White Ring Remover or Liberon Ring Remover. They often work but may change the sheen. If these fixes don't work, consult a pro to see what your other options are.

8. **Fill small cracks.** If you find nail holes or tiny cracks after applying the final finish, fill them with colored wax fill sticks, wax repair sticks or fill pencils, found at home centers and paint stores.

The directions tell you to rub the stick over the defect. But our pro recommends breaking off a chunk and warming it up in your hands. Then shape it to fit the flaw and press it in with a smooth tool. We used a 3/8-in. dowel with an angle on the end. For cracks, make a thin wafer, slide it into the crack and then work the wax in both directions to fill the crack. Buff with a soft cloth.

9. **Renew the luster with wipe-on finish.** The final step in your restoration project is to wipe on a coat of finish. After you clean your furniture piece and do any necessary repairs and stain touch-up, wiping on a coat of finish will restore the sheen and protect the surface. Any wipe-on finish will work; they're easy to put on with a rag. One coat is usually all you need to rejuvenate an existing finish.

To apply wipe-on finish, first put some on a clean rag. Apply it in a swirling motion as you would with car wax. Then wipe off excess finish, going in the direction of the grain. Let the finish dry overnight and you'll be ready to proudly display your furniture restoration project.

Iron-on edge banding

7/8" OAK EDGE BANDING

With a roll of wood veneer edge banding and a few simple tools, you can cover raw plywood edges so the plywood is nearly indistinguishable from solid wood. Iron-on edge banding is wood veneer with hot-melt adhesive preapplied to the back. You simply hold the edge banding in place, run over it with a household iron to heat the adhesive, let it cool and trim the edges flush. We'll show you how to do it and share some tips for getting perfect results every time. You'll find edge banding in common species like birch, oak and cherry at home centers and lumberyards. For exotic species and a greater variety of widths, search online or visit a specialty woodworking store. Rolls of edge banding come in lengths of 8 ft. to 250 ft. and widths of 13/16 in. to 2 in. For typical 3/4-in. plywood, buy 13/16- or 7/8-in.-wide edge banding.

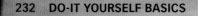

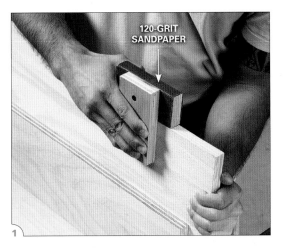

120-GRIT
SANDPAPER

1. **Clean up the edges.** Saw marks or other roughness will prevent a strong bond between the edge banding and the plywood. To avoid loose edge banding, sand the edges of the plywood smooth before you apply the edge banding. To keep from rounding edges while you sand, wrap a quarter sheet of 120-grit sandpaper around a small block of 3/4-in. plywood and screw another scrap to it as a guide. When the sandpaper starts showing signs of wear, remove the screw and reposition the sandpaper. After sanding, vacuum the edge to remove any dust.

"COTTON"
SETTING

ROLL
OF EDGE
BANDING

2. **Iron on the edge banding.** Use your regular clothes iron if you wish, but be aware that you may get adhesive on the metal baseplate. To be safe, buy a cheap iron from a thrift store or discount retailer. Be sure to empty any water out to avoid any steam and move the heat setting to "cotton." Use scissors to cut a length of edge banding about 1 in. longer than the edge you're covering. Starting at one end, center the edge banding with equal overhangs on each side and set the preheated iron at that end. Move the iron along the surface, keeping the edge banding centered with your other hand. Move the iron along at a rate of about 2 in. per second. The goal is to melt the adhesive without scorching the wood. Don't sweat it if you scorch or misalign the banding during application. Just run the iron over it again to soften the glue so you can peel the banding away. Cut yourself a new piece and start over.

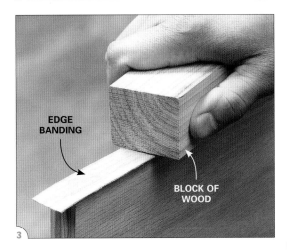

EDGE
BANDING

BLOCK OF
WOOD

3. **Press it while it's hot.** Make sure the edge banding is fully adhered by pressing

it down with a block of wood while it's still hot. Go back and forth over the edge a few times while the glue is cooling. Look for any areas that are raised. Heat those spots again and press them again with the block.

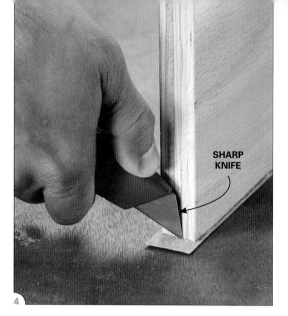

SHARP KNIFE

4. **Slice off the end**. The easiest way to remove the overhanging ends is to simply slice them off with a utility knife. Place the edge banding on a work surface and lightly score it a couple of times. Don't worry about cutting all the way through. Just lift the plywood and bend up the banding to snap it off.

5. **Use a trimmer on edges.** The quickest and easiest way to trim the edge banding flush to the plywood is with a special edge banding tool, such as the FastCap trimmer shown here.

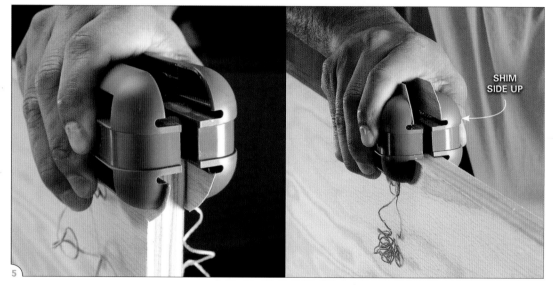

SHIM SIDE UP

Make a shallow pass first. Trim with the shimmed side first. Since less veneer is being removed with this side of the trimmer, the likelihood of runaway splits is greatly reduced. Start at one end and squeeze the trimmer until the shims are against the plywood. Then press down and slide the trimmer along the edge. Thin strips of veneer will peel away from both edges.

Flip the trimmer for the final pass. Flip the trimmer over and use the unshimmed side for a final trimming. When you're through, the edge banding should be almost perfectly flush with the plywood. If you missed any spots, just make another pass or two with the trimmer. The final sanding will remove the sharp edge and any remaining overhang.

GAP FOR BLADE

EDGE-BANDING SHIMS

DON'T

SPLICE

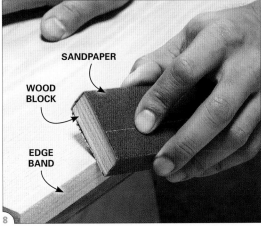

SANDPAPER

WOOD BLOCK

EDGE BAND

6. Modify your trimmer. Trimming the overhanging edges flush to the plywood without damaging the edge banding can be tricky. If the trimming blade catches in the wood grain, it can split the thin veneer and you'll have to start over. Prevent that headache by shimming one side of the trimmer with strips of edge banding so that it doesn't cut as deep. Just "tack" the shims on with the iron, making sure to leave a gap where the blades are. Since this trimmer has two cutting sides, you can leave the shims on one side to make the initial pass, and then just flip it over to make the final pass.

7. Don't leave a splice where it'll show. Splices can be hard to see on raw edge banding, but they may be highly visible after stain is applied. Inspect the edge banding before you cut it to length so you can cut around splices and avoid surprises later. Avoid waste by using spliced pieces in less visible areas.

8. Touch up with a sanding block. After you trim them, the edges will be sharp. Ease them with 150-grit sandpaper on a sanding block. Hold the sanding block at a slight angle and smooth out the edge. Sand gently and inspect the edge often to avoid sanding through the thin veneer.

Leveling

Whether you're hanging a picture or building a wall, getting things level is an important part of the project. And often there's a tip that'll help you get the job done quicker, easier or more accurately. Here are some of our favorites.

Poor man's laser level

If you need to make a long, level line and don't own a laser, try this method.

MARK TOP OF LEVEL

HEIGHT MARK

1. **Make a level mark.** Mark the desired height of your line on the wall. Hold your level at the mark and adjust it until the bubble is centered. Then make a mark at the opposite end of the level.

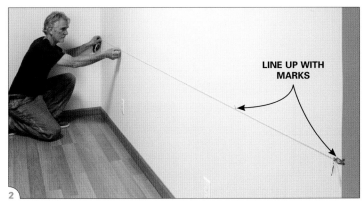

LINE UP WITH MARKS

2. **Snap a line.** Extend the line by stretching a chalk line and aligning it with both marks. If you're working indoors, use dust-off marking chalk, which is easy to erase. Stretch the chalk line and snap it to create a perfectly level line across the wall.

Smartphone level

Your phone can work like a small level. You can download a level app, or your phone may already have a leveling app built into the operating system. You wouldn't want to build a wall with a phone level, but it can come in handy for little leveling tasks around the house.

Extend your level

Extend your level with a straight board. Just remember to mark on the correct side of the level.

Fix crooked switches and outlets

Here's a handy tip! The screws that attach an outlet or a switch to the box go in a slot that allows the device to be adjusted. But you don't always have to remove the cover plate to fix crooked switches or outlets. Instead, try pushing a flat-blade screwdriver against the cover plate. Use a screwdriver with a sharp blade; a rounded-over blade will just slip off. You may have to push from more than one corner to fix really crooked devices.

Get your first row of tile perfectly level

Tubs and shower bases aren't always level, so starting your first row of tile against them could throw off your whole job. Instead, make level marks on the wall, line up the ends of a straight board with the marks and screw the board to the wall. Rest the first row of tile on the board for a perfectly level tile job. The distance from the top of the shower or tub to the top of the board should be less than the width of a tile. That way you can custom-cut the tiles to accommodate an out-of-level tub or shower and keep consistent grout lines.

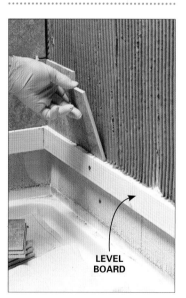

LEVEL BOARD

Check old levels before you use them

When levels get beaten up like this one, it's likely that some or all of the vials will be out of whack. And if you have a super-cheap or older level, don't trust it! Before you do any more leveling, test the vials for level (horizontal) and for plumb (vertical). Check the leveling vials by placing your level on a flat surface and piling playing cards under one end until the bubble is centered. Now lift the level and rotate it 180 degrees, end for end, and rest it on the cards in the same location. The bubble should still be centered. If it's not, your leveling vial is inaccurate. To check for accurate plumb vials, rest your level against a wall and note the location of the bubble between the lines (Photo 1). Then rotate the level 180 degrees, edge to edge, keeping the same end facing up (Photo 2). The bubble should be in the same spot. If not, your plumb vial is off. Levels like the one shown can be adjusted, but many levels can't. In some cases, one set of vials will be good, and you can simply cross out the bad set with a permanent marker to avoid using it. Or toss a bad level and buy a new one.

Rest the level against a corner. The bubble on this level is lined up with the right-hand line.

Put the opposite edge against the corner. Now the bubble on this level is lined up with the left-hand line, indicating a bad plumb vial. Adjust the level or mark this vial as bad with a permanent marker.

Fishing wire

Fishing wires and cables through finished walls can be tricky. You might be tempted to cut in a bunch of access holes, but you don't have to if you play it smart. With a few simple tools and these tips you can avoid a lot of drywall patching.

1. **Check the whole wall cavity with a stud finder.** A decent stud finder is a must-have for every wire-fishing job, but don't throw it back in your pouch after you've located the studs. Use your stud finder to check the whole wall cavity for obstacles. You don't want to find out the hard way that you should have fished your wire one stud cavity to the left or right.

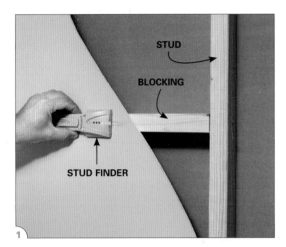

STUD

BLOCKING

STUD FINDER

1

pro tips!

➤ **Seal the holes.** If you're drilling holes through top and bottom plates or running wires through a fire wall in the garage, you must seal those holes with a fire-resistant caulk or foam sealant to comply with fire and energy codes. Fire-blocking insulated foam sealant is sold in cans at home centers and hardware stores.

2. **The tools you need.** Flex bits and glow rods are the go-to tools. Flex bits are great for drilling holes in hard-to-reach spaces. Buy a bit that has a hole on the end of it so you can use the bit itself to pull wires (more on that later).

Once your hole is drilled, you can shove a glow rod through the hole, attach your wire to the eyelet at the end and pull it back through. Glow rods can also be used to hook wires to pull them out. As their name suggests, glow rods glow in the dark. This makes them easier to spot when you're working in dark areas (which is most of the time).

Glow rods come in various lengths and thicknesses, and you can combine as many sections as the job requires. Thinner rods flex more and work better when you have to make sharp turns. A thicker rod can span longer distances and is better for hooking wires that are more than a few feet away.

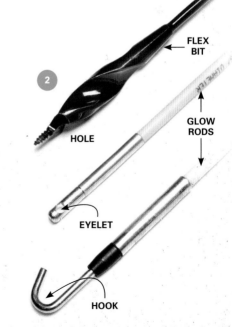

FLEX BIT

2

HOLE

GLOW RODS

EYELET

HOOK

3. **Push through more than you need.** When hooking a wire to pull it toward you, make sure there's more than enough wire to hook on to. Sometimes it's a real challenge to grab hold of a wire, and once you have it hooked, you don't want to lose it.

4. **Hook on to a flex bit.** Sometimes you don't need to use glow rods at all. Most flex bits have holes in the ends of them. If you have access to where the flex bit pops out, attach your wire directly to the bit and fish the wire through that way. Twist the wire and tape it up to make sure it doesn't come off when you're pulling it back through. Remove your bit from your drill before pulling so you don't accidentally spin the bit and twist up your wire.

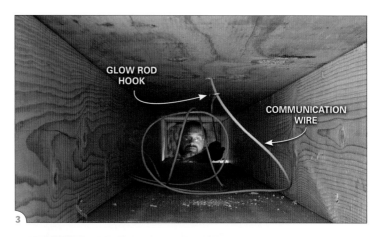

pro tips!

➤ **Buy extra wire.** Have plenty of extra wire or cable on hand, because it's not likely that you'll be able to fish a wire in a straight line from Point A to Point B. There's also the possibility that your wire might get hung up on something, and you'd have to abandon it and start over.

EXISTING CAN

GLOW ROD

5

MUD RING

6

5. **Fish wires through the holes for recessed lights.** When you're installing new recessed can lighting, fishing wires from one light to another is easy because you have a great big hole to pull the wires through. But even if you're not installing new lighting, you can use the existing openings. Many cans can be easily popped out of the opening by removing a few screws.

6. **Protect drywall with a mud ring.** Mud rings, also called drywall brackets or low-voltage "old-work" brackets, are great for protecting the drywall when you're drilling with a flex bit or cranking on a glow rod. They're easy to install (just tighten two screws) and inexpensive. Once the wires are connected, you can screw the wall plate to the mud ring. Mud rings are approved only for low-voltage wires like coaxial cables. If you need to install a box for an electrical receptacle or wall switch, install the mud ring temporarily to protect the drywall while you fish the wire, then remove it.

7. **Install conduit inside cabinets.** Additional outlets above the counter space is one of the most popular electrical retrofits. In this case, you can simply fish the wire through a flexible conduit installed right through the base cabinets. If you drill the holes for the conduit as far back and as high as you can, no one will ever notice.

CONDUIT

INSIDE BACK OF CABINET

7

8. **Get a better view with an inspection mirror.** You know your wire is in there somewhere, but you just can't seem to find it. It's probably hung up on another wire or pipe, but guessing isn't going to solve the problem. Shine a flashlight onto an inspection mirror to find out exactly what's going on. This is a simple, inexpensive tip that can save you a lot of time and frustration. Pick up an inspection mirror at an auto parts store.

FLASHLIGHT

INSPECTION MIRROR

8

9. **Don't spin the bit in insulation.** The best advice for fishing wires through insulation is "Avoid it if you can." The potential is always there to damage the vapor barrier or bunch up insulation, leaving cold spots in the wall. If you must fish wires through exterior walls, the best tip is to avoid spinning the flex bit until you make solid contact with the wood you plan to drill through. If you drill too early, you'll end up creating a large insulation cotton candy cone, which will make retrieving your bit difficult, if not impossible.

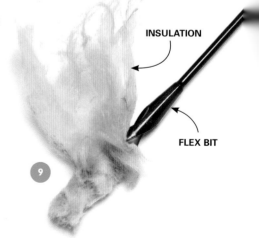

INSULATION

FLEX BIT

9

10. **Keep low-voltage wires away from electrical cables.** It's really tempting to fish low-voltage wires (like coaxial cable) through existing holes occupied by electrical cables, but don't do it! Even though cables are insulated, the high-voltage current can interfere with the signal in the low-voltage wires. This could result in bad TV reception or unreliable Internet service. Drill a new hole, and keep the new low-voltage wire several inches away from electrical cables. It's OK to run low-voltage wires perpendicular to cables, and it's also OK to run low-voltage wires next to electrical wires that are encased in conduit or metal sheathing.

11. **Invest in a Bumper Ball.** Wires aren't supposed to be installed any closer than 1-1/4 in. from a penetrable surface (the outside of the drywall). That means you shouldn't be drilling holes right next to the drywall. But it's not always easy to control where a flex bit goes. A Bumper Ball flexible drill bit guide installed on the end of your flex bit will help maintain the proper space between the bit and the outside of the wall cavity. You can buy a set of two at electrical suppliers or online.

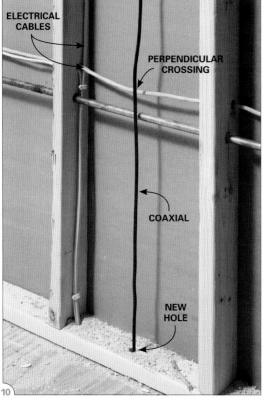

ELECTRICAL CABLES

PERPENDICULAR CROSSING

COAXIAL

NEW HOLE

10

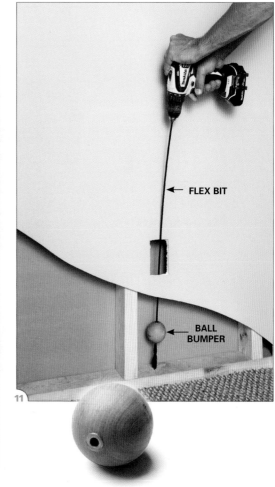

FLEX BIT

BALL BUMPER

11

Staining wood

Some types of wood, like pine, cherry, birch and maple, are notoriously difficult to stain. A board that has a nice, attractive grain pattern can end up with dark, splotchy areas after you apply the stain. But there's a simple way you can prevent most stain blotches.

Dark splotches show up when stain pigments become lodged in areas of grain that are more open. Unfortunately, it's not easy to tell which boards this will affect. One test is to wipe your board with mineral spirits. Spots that are prone to blotching show up darker. But the best test is to apply stain to a sample of the wood you're using. If the stain appears uneven or has unsightly dark areas, run the additional tests we show here to determine the best staining process.

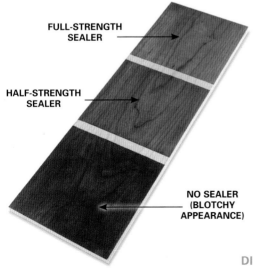

Step 1: Seal the wood before applying stain

Most stain manufacturers make prestain conditioners, but you'll get better results with the method shown here. A wipe-on oil finish was used as the sealer. The key is to apply a thin base coat to partially seal the wood before staining. Sanding sealers, dewaxed shellac and wipe-on finishes will all do the trick.

Some types of stain perform better than others on blotch-prone wood. In general, gel or heavy-bodied stains work best. Since these types of stain tend to have a high concentration of pigments, they also work better if you have to add several layers for a darker color (Step 2, p. 248). Just make sure the sealer and stain you're using are compatible. Using products from the same manufacturer is the safest bet.

Photo 1 shows how to make a test board with different concentrations of sealer. The concept is simple. The percentage of solids in the sealer determines how completely the pores in the wood are sealed. If the wood was sealed completely, it would be difficult to get any stain to stick. Diluting the sealer with mineral spirits allows you to experiment with different degrees of sealing. When you apply the stain (Photo 2), you'll see the results. Then you can choose the dilution rate that delivers the best results for your project.

Let the sealer dry for a few hours. Then sand the wood lightly with 220-grit paper before applying stain. An inexpensive turkey baster is a great tool for measuring small amounts of finish and mineral spirits. Mark the baster with a permanent marker. Just draw out equal amounts of sealer and solvent to make a 50 percent solution.

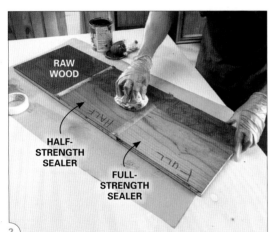

Step 2: Apply several coats of stain to get the desired shade

Start by making a test board with your chosen sealer concentration. Then stain the entire board. Let it dry and add a second layer of stain to all but one section. Repeat this process until you get to the desired color depth.

However, applying multiple coats of stain isn't always the best way to achieve a deeper color. For one thing, it'll take a long time to finish the project. You have to wait for each layer of stain to completely dry before adding the next. Otherwise, the new coat will dissolve the previous coat and you'll have a real mess on your hands. In fact, some stains will dissolve the stain below even if it is dry. (That's why testing is critical for a nice finish.) Another problem with multiple coats is that the stain will begin to obscure the natural grain. One solution is to opt for a less concentrated sealer. You'll get a bit more blotchy appearance, but the grain will show up better—a fair compromise.

ONE COAT OF STAIN

TWO COATS

THREE COATS

FOUR COATS

pro tips!

➤ **Seal pine before staining.** Dark stains on pine can look horrible. In addition to blotchiness, the softer areas between the grain lines soak up stain like a sponge, creating an unnatural look. This photo shows the dramatic difference between the raw and sealed areas of pine using the same stain color. Experiment with sealing the wood on your next pine project. You'll be amazed at the results.

STAINED WITHOUT SEALER

SEALED AND STAINED

ONE COAT OF STAIN

TWO COATS OF STAIN

THREE COATS OF STAIN

FOUR COATS OF STAIN

Step 3: Finish your test board to get the true effect

Treating your test board just like the finished project will give you a true representation of the final color and depth of the finish. Make sure you sand the test board with the same grit as you intend to use on your project. After you arrive at the desired degree of sealing and number of stain coats, apply the final clear finish to see how it looks. This is also a good time to test the effect of different sheens. Most finishes are available in sheens ranging from almost flat to high gloss. You'll be surprised at how much richer the stain looks after a coat of finish.

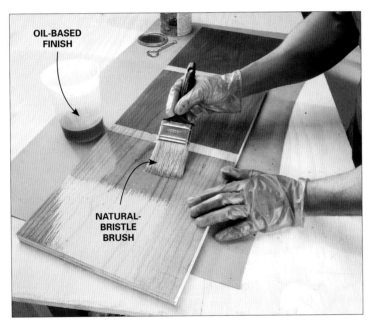

OIL-BASED FINISH

NATURAL-BRISTLE BRUSH

pro tips!

SEALED AND STAINED END GRAIN

➤ **Seal end grain.** End grain can look great and complement the board's surface, but it often ends up too dark. The solution is simple, though. Use the same prestain sealing method shown here to seal the end grain. You can also use this method on woods like oak that don't require a prestain sealer. Just be careful to sand off any sealer that gets on the face of the board before you stain.

END GRAIN STAINED WITHOUT SEALER

These expert carpenters spent years and years pounding hundreds of thousands of nails into just about anything made from wood. They built or worked on just about anything you can live in, park in, walk on, touch or see. The tricks and advice included here are some of the best of what they've learned on the job site.

From left, Spike Carlsen, Gary Wentz, Travis Larson and Jeff Gorton

Forget strings and stakes

You see it in print and on TV everywhere—some stake-and-board contraption set up to hold strings to help position postholes or to lay out footings or building footprints. But most of the time, there's a much better way. Tack together the construction lumber to outline the structure, square it up and use it as a giant template to do all your marking. Set it aside to do your digging and replace it to set the posts.— **Gary Wentz**

Easy framing formula

You don't need a math degree to estimate framing materials for walls. Here's a formula that works every time, no matter how many doors, windows or corners your walls have:

- ➤ One stud per linear foot of wall.
- ➤ Five linear feet of plate material (bottoms, tops and ties) per linear foot of wall.

It'll look like too much lumber when it arrives, but you'll need the extra stuff for corners, window and door frames, blocking and braces. Set aside the crooked stuff for short pieces.— **Gary Wentz**

Harness the power of a toenail

On my first job as a framing carpenter, I was beating on a stud to try to coax it into position. The stud just bounced back. A veteran framing carpenter walked over and drove a big nail at an angle through the edge of the stud. The last two hammer blows moved the stud into position, where it stayed. Now I use the toenail trick whenever I need to adjust stubborn lumber.— **Jeff Gorton**

11 best quick tips

1. Use blue chalk for your chalk lines unless you want permanent marks; then use red.

2. Save a couple of old circular saw blades. They're great for demo work like cutting through shingles, dirty wood or wood that may have hidden nails.

3. Don't waste all morning on extra lumber runs. Buy more than you need. You can always return the extra.

4. Utility knife blades are cheap. Replace them often, especially when cutting drywall.

5. Only buy carbide-tipped saw blades and router bits. They stay sharp for ages.

6. Don't skip the hearing protection. Even the occasional DIYer will lose some hearing from running loud power tools without it.

7. Measure twice, cut once. Oldest one in the book, but still true!

8. Spend a few extra bucks to buy a small box of every length of drywall screw there is. You'll use them for everything.

9. Invest in a stout, 1-in.-wide, 20- to 25-ft.-long tape measure. Throw the cheap flimsy one in the junk drawer.

10. Circular saw blades are cheap. Change them at the first hint of dullness.

11. Don't leave cutoffs lying all over the ground. Inevitably, you'll twist your ankle.

Throw together a miter saw bench

Whether you're working in your garage, out in the backyard or up at the cabin, take a few minutes and cobble together a miter saw bench. With a little creativity, you can use just about any materials you have on hand. The only custom work you'll need to do is to rip some spacer boards to make the outfeed support the same height as the saw table. It sure beats kneeling on the grass or perching the miter saw on horses. And the bench does double duty as a super-convenient work surface, too.— **Travis Larson**

pro tips!

➤ **Need a third hand?** It's surprising how inventive you can be when you have to work alone. One of the tricks I discovered is using a trim gun to tack up one end of the board while I go to the other end to mark the length or check the fit. If you have to take the board or trim piece down again, you'll only have one extra nail hole, which is easy to fill along with all the others.— **Jeff Gorton**

Memory (or lack thereof) trick

Stick masking tape to your tape measure for jotting down shapes and numbers. That way you won't forget the length on the way to the saw. — **Spike Carlsen**

pro tips!

Mark, don't measure

Early on in my carpentry career, I mismeasured an expensive baseboard and cut it too short. Instead of shouting, "You're fired," my boss just said, "Don't use your tape measure unless you have to." He was right. Holding trim in place and marking it is always more accurate than measuring, often faster and it eliminates mistakes. This is good advice for other types of carpentry work too, like siding, laying shingles and sometimes even framing. — **Gary Wentz**

Take a nip now and then

Keep a pair of nippers in your pouch whenever you're doing trim carpentry. When you pull trim from the wall, use them for pulling the nails through the back of the trim. — **Spike Carlsen**

Best all-purpose hammer

Whether you're doing rough construction or fine finish work, the best all-around hammer is a smooth-faced 20-ounce with a straight claw. I use the claw to drive it under walls for lifting, to embed it in framing and even to do extremely crude chiseling. But best of all, it's a better shape for pulling nails than the curved claw style. — **Spike Carlsen**

Nail safety

There was one must-do rule on my job sites. Don't ever let a board leave your hand if the sharp end of a nail is sticking out of it. They better be bent over or, better yet, pulled before that board hits the ground. Even with the edict, I still had to nurse foot punctures every now and then.

— **Travis Larson**

Best way to perfect miters

Fine-tuning a miter for a perfect fit is often a trial-and-error process. Practice on smaller test pieces until you get your miter saw set to exactly the right angle, then cut the actual parts. — **Gary Wentz**

Buy a trim gun

I haven't hand-nailed a piece of interior trim in 25 years. Why? Because air-powered trim guns make the results so much faster, better and neater. No splits, no predrilling, no knocking the piece out of place as you hammer, and only itty-bitty holes to fill. — **Travis Larson**